P. 60

The Humanity of God

The
Humanity of God

AN INTERPRETATION OF THE
DIVINE FATHERHOOD

By

John Wright Buckham, D.D.

Author of "Mysticism and Modern Life," "Progressive
Religious Thought in America," "Personality
and Psychology," Etc.

New York and London

Harper & Brothers Publishers

1928

THE HUMANITY OF GOD
COPYRIGHT, 1928, BY HARPER & BROTHERS
PRINTED IN THE U.S.A.
FIRST EDITION
K-C

▼

TO

DANJO EBINA, D.D., LL.D.

PRESIDENT OF DOSHISHA UNIVERSITY

AND TO THE ALUMNI OF

PACIFIC SCHOOL OF RELIGION
IN JAPAN

THIS VOLUME IS INSCRIBED

IN CHRISTIAN AFFECTION

AND ESTEEM

✠

Contents

Preface

ONE who, like the writer, seldom fails to read the preface of a book does so, presumably, hoping to find in it some inkling of the reason why the author has dared to add one more to the appalling accumulation of literary débris of all sorts which lies like a heavy nightmare upon the breast of a long-suffering literate humanity. Yet it is but rarely that a preface furnishes anything more than a conventional acknowledgment of indebtednesses and the expression of a modest hope on the part of the author that his volume will be not only contributive to the expert in its field but interesting and instructive to the lay reader. Contrast such prefaces with the communicative introductions and "preliminaries" of Sir Walter Scott or the "Before the Curtain" of *Vanity Fair!*

Doubtless the marked hesitation on the part of most authors to talk about themselves is the chief cause of this prefatorial reticence; and this is considerate and commendable. But one does not need to be dumb in order not to be garrulous. A *via media* is surely discoverable. Occasionally one finds throughout an entire volume an opening of the heart to the reader on the part of a reserved author, like Hawthorne, which is as grateful as it is surprising and leads the reader to part with it reluctantly, moved by sympathy and understanding.

The author of a volume with a title such as this may well suspect that questions will arise in the mind of the reader, however well-disposed, which stand in the way of complete confidence. One such is prompted by the nature of the subject. It runs, subconsciously perhaps, somewhat thus: Since such a task as is here attempted has so great inherent difficulties, why venture upon it? *Ambulando solvitur.* Why not be content with simple belief in God as Heavenly Father and let the questions which arise in connection with it alone? The answer is: Because these questions will not let *us* alone. The modern mind is not content with the attitude of acceptance. For better, for worse, it has set out on a persevering quest of truth. This adventure should be honored, even if it leads to insoluble difficulties or to a realm of mystery which neither theology nor philosophy can penetrate very far.

Another query will doubtless occur to many readers. It is one which has again and again crossed the path of the author, like a forbidding spectre: *Would you be writing thus affirmatively and convincedly of the Divine Fatherhood had your life been so hedged about with limitations and darkened with troubles and sorrows as that of most of your fellow-men? Have you taken adverse facts sufficiently into account?* This question, I confess, makes me pause. I am not at all sure that I can answer it with sufficient detachment, having more reason

than most men to believe gratefully in the Divine Goodness. And yet, looking back across more than threescore
years, filled with advantage and opportunity and all manner of good, memory tells me that, after all, life has not
always run like a quiet stream between full banks, or
been wholly exempt from a share in those adversities and
perplexities that make the Fatherhood of God seem sometimes a remote and impossible fancy. Nor have the woes
of my fellows left me untouched by troubling questions.
No one who has lived through the dark years of the Great
War, even though he were neither in the trenches nor in
Leavenworth prison, but must have been often haunted
by doubt of the Divine Goodness; and the aftermath of
the War has been hardly less severe upon one's faith in
God and man.

Yet in the midst of these ambushes of doubt and dismay there have not failed the Great Book of strength
and the grace of One who has power to restore youth and
hope to an exhausted world. Everywhere, too, even on
Main Street, are faces that have not gathered darkness
and friends whose very presence is reassurance. Best of
all, at my side has been one whose tenderness and love
and unfailing charm I cannot account for except as one
of those perfect gifts that are from Above. Nor can one
who has walked beneath forest trees and followed sing-
ing streams and listened to the song-sparrow and the
hermit thrush and caught sight of wild flowers blooming
in quiet places and looked up at the stars quite lose confidence that at the heart of the universe there is Love.

Not without becoming *still,* may one know. Also I have
noted that it is not those who have suffered most and had
least of the good things of life that have had most doubt
of the Fatherhood of God.

The book was commenced as a series of lectures for
the Divinity School of Doshisha University, Japan. Post-
ponement of the privilege of visiting that alluring land
obliges the author to content himself with dedicating it to
friends in Japan whom he expected to see. He does this
with the greatest pleasure, hoping the volume may help
in promoting those friendly relations between truth
seekers in the two countries which mean so much and
which have sprung, one may well believe, from a common
spiritual kinship to One God and Father of all.

A number of the chapters were read to a Seminar in
Pacific School of Religion made up of students just out
of, or still within, the University atmosphere. The breadth
of vision and earnestness with which the members of the
Seminar entered into the consideration of the subject
leads me to hope that such a treatment of it as is here
presented will be not unwelcome to younger as well as
older minds. I have embodied in the text and footnotes
several contributive sentences from the papers presented
by members of the Seminar. To the authors and publishers of the works from which extracts have been made
I am greatly indebted, and most of all to the men and
women whose lives have helped to make the Fatherhood
of God a vital reality.

The reader who is not interested in the philosophical

aspects of the subject can easily select from the titles, the chapters which have to do with its more concrete treatment.

A word may be in order concerning the somewhat miscellaneous literary form of the volume. If the reader should find himself wondering at times whether he is reading philosophy or theology, essay or treatise, observation or speculation, dissertation or homily, prose or poetry, I hope he may conclude that there is something of all these in my book. For the treatment of such a theme requires them all—and more. The Divine Fatherhood is not a subject merely for Sunday School instruction or class-room study or hortatory apologetic, but for free, thorough and comprehensive discussion and interpretation, aided by all the resources one can command. Therefore the author has used without hesitation the wide privileges of so expansive a theme and varied the treatment from page to page, and chapter to chapter, trusting that the reader will humor him in this, thinking as he follows the somewhat extended course of the discussion:

> "Perhaps it may turn out a song
> Perhaps turn out a sermon,"

or even a contribution to the philosophy of religion. At any rate it is my hope that at the close, an old, well-thought, well-loved and well-lived faith may have been made a little freer from doubt and difficulty.

Before closing this prefatory word I desire to express my gratitude to the authors whose works are quoted herein, and to the publishers of their respective volumes, to my colleagues in the faculty of the Pacific School of Religion, and to Professor George Herbert Palmer, Dr. O. W. S. McCall and Rev. Hugh V. White for interest and assistance.

The original title chosen for this volume was, *The Fatherhood of God and the Modern Mind.* It seemed to me a fairly good title, but while searching for a better —under the wise instigation of the Religious Book Editor of my honored Publishers—I came upon the following sentence in that challenging volume by H. R. L. Sheppard, *The Impatience of a Parson:* "Doubtless the outstanding contribution which Jesus Christ made to religion was His belief in the goodness and availability of God, Who was to Him and to all men in the relationship of a Father. If our Lord revealed the divinity of man, He most certainly also revealed the humanity of God." "The *humanity of God,*"—here, I perceived at once, was the title I had been looking for, expressing in a warmer and more vivid way the conception of God which the book endeavors to present,—while not out of keeping with an attempt to relate this conception to the characteristic attitudes and difficulties of the modern mind. In adopting it I desire to acknowledge a sense of indebtedness to Dr. Sheppard which none but he who has searched diligently for book titles can appreciate.

JOHN W. BUCKHAM.

PACIFIC SCHOOL OF RELIGION,
  Berkeley, California

PART I

Interpretations

Experiencing God

Personal Theism, symbolized by the Fatherhood of God, the best Interpretation of Religious Experience and the most rational Theory of Man and the Cosmos—The Emotional Element in Religion arising from an Experience of the Numinous—The Cognitive Element—The Volitional Element, or Faith—Expression, Interpretation and Description all involved in Religious Experience; Theology as the Interpretation of Religion—A Name for God itself an Interpretation; the Search for the Best Name.

THE depreciators of theology—whose name is legion —who chance to see the title of this volume will probably regard it as one more defense of a long accepted but now tottering Christian dogma. That is not its intention, nor, I trust, its character. Its purpose, instead of being defensive, is, rather, to maintain that *the symbolic conception of God as Father offers an interpretation of religious experience and a theory concerning the ultimate meaning of man and the cosmos which is not only tenable but is more rational as well as more productive of human well-being than any other.*

I

So long has the habit of evading the real issues involved in the doctrine of the Fatherhood of God prevailed
and so inadequate have been many of the attempts to
defend it, that it is hard for open minds to conceive the
possibility that this faith has any other grounds than
those of sentiment, safety and tradition. The intellectual
principles of Philosophical Theism are still respected, but
to go from the philosophical ideas of an Infinite Being,
World-Ground, First Cause, or Eternal Energy, to Divine
Fatherhood is often regarded as a descent to a lower
level, a concession to the average mind which needs an
anthropomorphic conception of Deity for comfort and
support.

In contrast to this concessive and merely sentimental
evaluation of the Fatherhood of God the position here
maintained is *that Personal Theism as symbolized in
Divine Fatherhood is as good as any other philosophy
of the universe—and better;* as good because it presents
a theory of reality and value which accounts for the facts
of human experience and the nature of the world we live
in more reasonably than any other; better because it
betters those who hold it—offering them a practical working principle which sweetens, greatens and harmonizes
life as nothing else does. But while this is the thesis of
the volume, the method proposed is that of enquiry rather
than of dogmatic assertion.

It would seem best to begin, then, by going down into the roots of religion far enough to gain some idea of its nature and validity, to discover how the idea of God itself arose and developed toward the Ethical Monotheism which ripened into Divine Fatherhood as taught by Jesus.

II

As a result of thorough, unprejudiced and prolonged study, religion is now recognized as a normal human experience—pervasive, persistent, practically universal. The most noticeable and outstanding feature of this experience is its emotional character. The feeling element is uppermost.

Religious emotion may perhaps best be described as due to the sense of sacredness. Rudolf Otto has termed it the *numinous*, holding that it is "perfectly *sui generis* and irreducible to any other."[1] But though *sui generis* it is not detached from experience as a whole.[2]

[1] *The Idea of the Holy*, p. 7.

[2] Henry Nelson Wieman in his stimulating volume *Religious Experience and Scientific Method* writes: "When the total object of all our experience becomes for us an object of contemplation, we discern that which stirs us deeply, that which awakens in us the religious attitude" (p. 74). This is as ambiguous as it is suggestive. What is meant by the object of all our experience? In answer to a letter of inquiry Professor Wieman allows me to quote the following reply: "In general my point is that all experience is experience of some object or other beyond the person who undergoes the experience. Consequently all experience, taken as a totality, is the experience of something which, taken as a totality, could be called an object. God is to be sought in this objective totality. Whether he is identical with that totality, or some phase of it, is a question which I leave undetermined in this book, since my sole concern in it is to indicate the relation between religious

Religion, even in its crude and semiprimitive forms, is a recognition of Something over and above what may be seen and touched, something supersensible. Before this *Something* men bow; to it they sacrifice; for it they build fanes and temples, and for its sake, not seldom, they are willing to suffer and to die. A great part of all this homage may be foolish and irrational, but it is at least a tribute, as well as a testimony, to what later generations have called Spirit, the Eternal, God.

Such homage, however crude or even diabolical, has raised men above the animal and above themselves. The very effort and cost of it testifies to and fosters a higher nature in man, in process of self-realization.

With the sense of the sacred, which may be regarded as the soul of primitive religion, were blended many other experiences and motives of an individually and socially protective and self-seeking sort. The preservation of life in which Professor G. F. Moore finds the essence of religion, the belief in spirits of which Tylor makes so much, the *quid pro quo* element in sacrifice and prayer which so frequently characterizes primitive religion, the element of social utility, which the Durkheim School regards as the very substance of religion, have

experience and scientific method." In Dr. Wieman's later volume, *The Wrestle of Religion with Truth* (1927) he defines the formal concept of God as follows: "Very briefly, God is that feature of our total environment which most vitally affects the continuance and welfare of human life" (p. 14). That this feature of the environment is Personal does not appear, although it is not excluded according to the terms of the definition. (See the criticism of the writer and the reply of Dr. Wieman in *The Christian Century*, February 23, 1928.)

all undoubtedly played a part, and a very large part, in religion. Yet when all these and other factors have been allowed their full place there remains, over and above, Something which escapes, exceeds, transcends them. And this Something more, whether real or imaginary, may be regarded as the soul of religion.

Strangely, variously, often weirdly and repulsively, this "numinous" element in religion has manifested itself, baffled by perverting hostile environment, intermingled with other forms of experience, but gradually finding itself, purifying itself, understanding itself, until from Mana and Orenda it begins to ascend to the One, the Righteous, the Holy, the Good, the Perfect, "our Father who art in Heaven."

It is a long road from the superstition of the savage— startled at the sight of his totem, alternately bowing to or belaboring his fetish, prostrating himself before the rising sun, uttering his wild cries in the war dance—to the silent worship of a Friends' meeting; from the coarseness of cannibals, devouring their victim that they may absorb something of his prowess, to the celebration of the Lord's Supper; from the crude anticipation of the Amerind burying his implements with the dead chieftain to the pure inspiration of an Easter morning or the refined reasoning of an Ingersoll lecture on immortality. Nevertheless, there is a thread of continuity, however faint and broken, running from the one to the other. It lies in the recognition of, and the impulse to get into harmony with, the supersensible, the spiritual, "the Beyond that is within."

III

Feeling is not the only element in religion. Cognition also has a place and part. Beside the feeling of sacredness there is in the religious experience an *awareness* of Something or Some One beside oneself present in the experience and associated with the emotion. This is *knowledge*.[3] It is true that the knowledge does not readily emerge into definiteness. The sense of the sacred may be very strong, yet very hazy and ill-defined as to its object. The experient may not succeed in distinguishing what is felt from the feeling itself, and yet be aware that *the reality is not an outward object but Something associated with the object*. The sun-worshiper, for example, while he centers his adoration on the orb of day, may at the same time be dimly conscious that he is worshipping Somewhat, or Some One, transcending or pervading the sun, rather than the sun itself. The savage sometimes names this sacred Somewhat *Mana, Orenda, Manitou*, or describes it as a spirit dwelling in his fetish, thus giving it an acknowledged existence and character of its own. He worships his fetish not as itself potent, but as the abode of potency. His totem in some mysterious way embodies the spirit of the tribe. Very vivid is this sense of Energy or Power in the savage mind.

[3] Cf. W. B. Selbie: *The Psychology of Religion*, p. 52 ff.

"Thoughtful Bantu," writes Edwin W. Smith, "would echo Carlyle: 'Force, everywhere Force! We ourselves a mysterious force. . . .' "[4]

Frequently the worshiper *personifies* the sun, the moon, the star, seeing therein, perhaps, the deified hero, or the dimly recognized god. He thus worships the heavenly bodies not as mere objects, but as enveloped in a supernatural halo which invests them with a quality of sacredness. One of the most eminent Christian leaders of Japan, President Danjo Ebina of the Doshisha University, in relating his youthful experience as a sun-worshiper, has described to me how he greeted the rising sun with gratitude and awe. Yet even then, he added, he recognized in the sun something transcending it which he later found in Him "in whose light we see Light."

This Somewhat, or Some One, is not at first regarded as ethical or truly spiritual. Its sacredness is often more magical than spiritual. It begets dread, dismay, fear, as well as fascination. Not until the whole range of human life and thought has been raised to a higher level does the sacred become sacred indeed, purified, moralized, spiritualized.

The cognitive factor in religious experience may be best described as *intuition, i.e.,* direct insight or recognition. This intuitive power of recognition is implicit in the untrained human mind, but becomes clearer with advancing mental, moral, and spiritual growth.[5]

[4] *The Religion of Lower Races,* p. 10.

[5] In making intuition a part of the religious experience itself—thus assuring its rationality—and the explication of it a function of interpre-

IV

The gradual purification and spiritualization of the religious sentiment reveals another of its characteristic qualities. Present in it are not only emotional and cognitive elements, but also an active outreach of soul or *faith.* Volition is involved. He that cometh, not simply to the true God, but to any god, must believe that He is and that He is the rewarder of them that diligently seek Him. Faith is in itself a beneficial, strengthening form of inner activity. As a positive and vital attitude it tends to relate its possessor earnestly and actively to life, in spite of the fact that when it is misdirected toward malevolent deities or demons it gives rise to dread and superstition and all manner of ills.

Thus religion, in all its stages and manifestations, witnesses to man's consciousness of a supermaterial order. Something, or Some One—Mana, Orenda, Manitou, a God, or gods, or spirits,—superior to, though intimately associated with, the objects and persons by which he is surrounded, presses in upon him. That this realm is peopled by him with creations of fancy does not mean that itself is a creation of fancy.

Whatever may be the explanation of religion, nothing is more inherently, characteristically, significantly *human.*

---

tation, or theology, it is not intended to depreciate the intellectual factor. Bishop Temple has put the matter well as regards the existence of God: "The true case for Theism does not rest upon general philosophy alone, nor upon religious experience alone, but upon the coincidence or convergence of these two." *Christ the Truth,* p. 117.

The biologist, the anthropologist, the behaviorist, may explain it in terms of the struggle for existence, or of social relationships, or of psycho-physical 'reactions. Doubtless these are factors in religion, but they are not sufficient to account for the fact of religion itself—either its rise, its development or its consummation. They are useful as descriptions of the religious experience on its functional side, but they do not come within sight of religion itself.[6] The sense of sacredness, involving an awareness of a genuine, though but partially apprehended reality, remains one of the ultimate, significant, irresolvable factors of human experience, however closely bound up with experience as a whole.

V

Religious experience gives birth to two natural products, expression and interpretation. It is essential to its nature to embody itself in outward act and also in thought.

Religion has three forms of expression—creed, cult, and conduct. The creed is the expression, in a common assertive act, of the rational content of religious experience. Worship is its expression in fitting, symbolic outer form. Conduct is the expression of the experience in practical everyday activity in keeping with the sacred

[6] For the psychology of religion the reader may consult J. B. Pratt, *The Religious Consciousness*, W. B. Selbie, *The Psychology of Religion*, George A. Coe, *The Psychology of Religion*, and the writer's *Religion as Experience*.

character of the experience itself. In the higher religions this activity becomes moral.

Religious experience also prompts and requires interpretation. Otherwise it is incoherent and impotent. Experience—interpretation: these are at once distinguishable and inseparable. They are simultaneous and interpenetrating, affecting one another, as do soul and body. Yet they should not be confounded. Always experience is fundamental, primary; interpretation, derivative and secondary. And yet, interpretation is essential, and invaluable, and is already present potentially in the experience.

Interpretation should be distinguished from still another attendant of experience—description. Description is a dramatization of experience. An experience may be described without interpreting it. Description relates, narrates, pictures, an experience; interpretation probes into its meaning and relationships and brings them out. Expression, on the other hand, *voices* an experience, gives it emotional utterance, but neither describes nor interprets it. Worship and art express and to that extent describe religion, but do not, strictly speaking, interpret it.

Interpretation may be very limited, sluggish, inaccurate, misleading; or it may be proximately just, discerning, discriminating, thus giving to the experience itself heightened value and meaning. Two persons may have much the same experience and describe and express it in much the same way, and yet interpret it so diversely as to find themselves in open disagreement. This fact lies at the root of most of the bitterness, misunderstanding, and strife that has darkened the history of religion. For it is in the realm of theology that conflict occurs; *i.e.*, in the interpretation of religion. Theology succeeds at best only very imperfectly. That experience should outrun interpretation is quite what we should expect.

What is this insistent yet elusive religious experience that grasps men, yet that they cannot wholly grasp; that is now so real and again so unreal; that visits one, now in lonely moments, now among those who are "all with one accord in one place"; that cheers, rebukes, eludes, yet will not let us go? How can we expect this Undine to be caught and imprisoned, this most vital yet intangible reality to be analyzed, measured, classified, understood? Yet to leave it uninterpreted would be to suppress and dishonor it. All that can be done is to interpret it in the best terms to be found; never imagining that these are adequate nor attempting to force them upon others. Thus will theology again become plastic, vital, variant, as it is in the New Testament itself.

VI

Much may be learned of the various ways in which men have interpreted the Central Reality of religious experience by the names which they have given to It. For every significant name is itself an interpretation;—an idea crystallized in a word. Often it sums up long periods of cumulative experience and thought. A name for God is not a mere designation of an individual, as is the name of a man. It is a concept, and at the same time a descriptive and personal term. As a rule a divine name seizes upon some prominent aspect of the experienced reality to the exclusion of all others. In this way it secures definiteness, although at the expense of comprehensiveness.

To rehearse but a portion of the names which have been given to the object of religious experience is to disclose at once the fecundity of the experience itself and the multiformity yet insufficiency of the interpretations attached to It: Mana, Orenda, Manitou, Shang Ti, Tao, Heaven, All-Fadir, the One Above, Creator, Power, Intelligence, the One, the All, the Absolute, the Unmoved Mover, the Infinite, the Eternal, Mind, Spirit, the Good, God, Mystery, Atman, the Self, Other Mind, the Power not ourselves, the Unknowable, the First Cause, the World Ground, Principle, the Almighty, the All-Merciful, Love, Light, Life, Truth, the Beyond that is within, the Great Companion, Our Father in Heaven. The Koran well calls God the One of the Ninety-nine Beautiful Names.

As one glances through such an array of names he is struck by three things regarding them. (1) There is none of them but that may not, in some sense, be attached to the Spiritual Presence which presses in upon human consciousness. (2) Nevertheless, consistency requires that if certain of these names be true interpretations others can be accepted only in an accommodated sense—

e.g., if God is the Creator He cannot be the All, if He is the Absolute He cannot—strictly speaking—be the Father, if He is the Unknowable He cannot be Truth. (3) While most if not all of these names predicate something that may be true of God, they are not all of the same worth. Among them there may well be one that is *best*—one that compresses the nature of spiritual reality into a word so replete and moving, so vital, and sufficing, that it manifests its inherent superiority and fitness above all others. Is there such a name?

In "Our Father" a name for God has been chosen and consecrated—by the religion that has come to be the most widely influential of all—which may well prove to be the most inherently adequate, moving and expansive, name possible. Into the meaning and validity of this name we are to look.

CHAPTER I

Can the Modern Mind Retain the Belief in God as Father?

Faith in the Fatherhood of God widely questioned in our Time; due largely to the strongly Scientific and Critical Habit of the Modern Mind—Practical Materialism also characteristic of our Age—Yet these Negative Attitudes are offset by the present Tendency in Evolutionary Theory toward the Recognition of Purpose—Metaphysical *vs.* Metaphorical Terms for God—Chief Reason why the Name *Father* represents the best possible Conception of Deity.

FAITH in the Fatherhood of God is a heritage which the Christian of to-day cherishes with reverence and affection, but at the same time with not a little concern. He is confident that it is not only in itself an ennobling and beneficial belief but essential to Christianity. "Whatever else Christianity may believe in," writes a modern-minded Christian leader, "it must believe in God, Father of all men." [1] Yet many a Christian is not sure that he can continue to hold this faith with mental integrity in the face of all the facts which seem to contradict it.[2] It is only the very immature, or the very

[1] Harry Emerson Fosdick: *A Christian Conscience about War*, p. 7.
[2] This is indicated in the title of William Newton Clark's admirable volume answering the inquiry: *Can I Believe in God, the Father?*

mature, Christian who is untroubled by questionings concerning it. As for the man outside the Christian pale, to him the idea of a Fatherly God is apt to seem purely *naïve*, at variance with modern knowledge and quite out of touch with modern life.

I

It is not difficult to account for this attitude of hesitation. It is the product, in large part at least, of "the modern mind." The modern mind is shaped, controlled, saturated by science; and the scientific mind finds it difficult to make room for such a universal affirmation as that of the Fatherhood of God, unsupported by conclusive scientific evidence.[3]

The enormous progress made by natural science, while it registers a great advance in human achievement, has begotten in our age a sense of superiority based upon an appreciation of scientific methods and results, which is hardly warranted by a just estimate of comparative values. The proportionate emphasis upon scientific, as contrasted with religious and philosophic, interests is well illustrated in the space given to these respective subjects in that representative modern work, the eleventh edition of the Encyclopaedia Britannica. Examples of the disproportion, chosen somewhat at random, follow: *Brahmanism* twelve columns *vs. Brewing* sixteen columns

[3] The "modern mind" is used in the sense of the contemporary mind. By "science" is meant *natural science,* although in its broader meaning —as Paul Canes rightly insisted—*science* includes all ordered knowledge.

(including illustrations); *Church* seven columns (*Church History* thirty columns) *vs. Climate* thirty-three columns; *Ethics* seventy columns *vs. Electricity* (including its applied forms) one hundred forty-six columns; *Jesus Christ* twenty-two columns *vs. Infinitesimal Calculus* fifty-one columns; *Poetry* twenty-eight columns *vs. Plants* one hundred eight columns; *Mohammedan Religion* fourteen columns *vs. Magnetism* sixty-four columns; *Personality* one and one-half columns *vs. Iron and Steel* sixty-eight columns; *Philosophy* ten columns *vs. Planarians* thirteen columns; *Religion* twenty-nine columns (including illustrations) *vs. Reptiles* eighty-three columns; *Sin* one column *vs. Skull* twelve columns; *Soul* no article *vs. Sound* thirty-six columns.[4]

Scientific knowledge is of incalculable worth, spiritual as well as practical, yet it is a narrow estimate which regards it as superior to the culture of imagination, or looks upon its achievements as greater than those of poetry, art, philosophy or religion.

To assert that science has been given an undue proportionate emphasis in our time is not to disparage the scientific mind or to pronounce it irreligious. Indeed, in its thoroughness, its patience, its sincerity, it is not only admirable, but, in its own way, also religious. It is only when science leads to the disparagement, or ignoring, of moral and spiritual values that it becomes inimical

---

[4] The Britannica, one does not need to say, is an extremely comprehensive book of knowledge and has many notable articles on religious topics. In its proportionate emphases, it simply reflects, as do other encyclopedias, the mind of our time.

to the highest human interests; and that occurs only when it has suffered inflation. It is quite evident as Graham Wallis has said, that "men have recently increased their power over Nature without increasing the control of that power by thought." [5]

To say that the modern mind is scientific does not imply that it is a closed mind but only that it is not widely comprehensive. Openness of mind is a characteristic of science; so also is humility, but it is not easily maintained when achievement succeeds achievement as has been the case with science since the middle of the last century. Nineteenth-century science, although its greatest exponent was so humble a man as Charles Darwin, came to assume, at one time, a decidedly self-sufficient and dogmatic tone. Its victories were almost too great to be borne with equilibrium. Experience has taught the science of to-day to be more hesitant and open-minded. Too many revisions of former hypotheses have become necessary, too many incursions of unsuspected forces and factors have occurred, to permit the science of to-day to indulge in theology's favorite vice of dogmatism. It has learned, to some degree, the lowliness of true knowledge. The scientific mind at its best has an enviable degree of reserve of judgment, of hospitality to new truth, of readiness to revise conclusions, and of the grace of humility.[6] But the scientific interest is confined to the natural world

[5] *The New Republic,* June 16, 1926, p. 118.
[6] "It is the part of painstaking science to contribute humility to religion, to keep us receptive to new truth." Robert A. Millikan, Commencement Address at Oberlin College, 1926.

and is accompanied sometimes by a strongly positivistic note in philosophy.

The modern mind is also intensely and unsparingly *critical*. Criticism is not a new activity of the human mind, but it is safe to say that it never has attained to such a degree of penetration and thoroughness, nor invaded so many fields, as at the present time. Modern criticism is eminently thorough and incisive, but it is wanting in the spirit of *appreciation*—the sympathetic recognition of truth, merit, virtue, wherever they are to be found—which characterizes the highest form of criticism. Lacking this spirit it has unhesitatingly shattered the false idols of the past without being sufficiently aware of the *ideals* which are often closely bound up with them.

It should not be forgotten that true ideals are sometimes attached to mistaken ideas. One may instance the ennobling influence which that blundering and now despised book, Deems' *Life of George Washington*, had upon the mind of the youthful Abraham Lincoln. Here was a factually inaccurate and misleading biography nevertheless producing a wholesome effect—evidence that the ideal may be true and work its ends even if the facts with which it is associated are incorrect. The disillusioning biography has become a familiar and widely read form of literature; but disillusionment may be carried so far as to miss the virtue which underlies weakness and the wheat hidden in the chaff.

Criticism, as it is witnessed to-day, fearlessly searching every form of belief, theory, and practice, is to be welcomed and furthered—until it transcends its limits, becomes skeptical and cynical and proves "procuress to the lords of hell."

II

To describe the present period as scientific and critical is not exhaustive. It has another conspicuous characteristic—largely the result of *applied* science, but by no means its fault. I refer to the practical materialism, the absorption in the outer to the neglect of the inner life, which is everywhere apparent and which is vitiating what has been dubbed our "jazz age." This practical materialism is accompanied by an absorbing *hedonism*, the reverse side of which is either religious indifference or a hopeless determinism. Reviewing several representative contemporary novels, a discerning critic remarks: "The authors are not engaging existence; they are rather in full flight from it. There are no longer problems to be solved; there are merely facts to be accepted or avoided." [7] The discipline of science is offset by popular absence of restraint, open-mindedness by no-mindedness, eagerness for truth by indifference. This superficial attitude renders such a belief as the Fatherhood of God to many minds alien and unwelcome, neither credible nor desirable.

Here, then, is a situation confusing, disquieting, and all too far unfaced: a Christian mind, committed to belief

[7] Walter Miller in *Survey Graphic,* December, 1925, p. 312.

in God the Father as the central article of its faith, yet increasingly conscious of the difficulties involved in it; a scientific mind open and earnest, but not concerned greatly with moral and spiritual values and therefore disposed to allow the thought of God, with all that it means to human life, to drop out of sight; a popular mind, disinclined to unselfish living or serious thinking and without the restraints and incentives of an earlier Christian faith. One cannot face a situation like this with complacency. Yet this is not the whole story. In spite of these negative influences, there is evidence of an earnest desire, on every hand, for a unified, reassuring conception of the meaning of life and of the universe and for a form of faith which will support such a conception.

III

As if to meet this desire for a more reassuring interpretation of life and the world, there has arisen a very marked tendency in present-day scientific-philosophic theory toward the recognition of the presence of directive Purpose in the universe.[8] The leading exponent of this point of view is Professor C. Lloyd Morgan in his Gifford Lectures, *Emergent Evolution* (First Series) and *Life, Mind, and Spirit* (Second Series). In the chapter on Divine Purpose in the latter series, Dr. Morgan writes as follows:

[8] Cf. Lawrence Henderson, *The Order of Nature;* J. Arthur Thompson, *The System of Animate Nature;* J. G. Simpson, *Man and the Attainment of Immortality.*

According to emergent evolution we find and loyally accept a series of ascending steps in advance as we pass from natural entities of lower to those of higher status; and in the evolution of that which we deem the highest of natural entities, a man, these steps afford instances of a determinate plan which includes the evolutionary progress of all relevant events in him, alike in physical and in mental regard. . . .

With respect to the concept of the supernatural there is a valid sense, though not the commonly accepted sense, in which on our principles we may speak of any newly emergent character as supernatural in that it is a step beyond that which is within the order of nature up to date. In this sense the advent of life, of reflective reference often identified with mind, of that which I distinguish as a spiritual attitude, are successive instances of the supernatural. But when they do come they are no longer *in this sense* supernatural. I have spoken of them as successively supervenient. Regarded as instances of Divine Purpose, I find difficulty in the concept of Divine *intervention*. For if *all* advance in nature be a manifestation of Divine Purpose, on what understanding can the Divine "intervene" at any stage of that manifestation?

This, however, does not touch the quick of what most people mean by the supernatural. The word commonly carries a different connotation. The implication here is that the natural and the supernatural belong to wholly diverse orders of being. . . . There is for me (I must repeat) one and only one realm of reality that *is both natural and spiritual,* in ultimate unity of substance, but *is not both natural and supernatural* if this imply ultimate diversity of orders of being.

This is a very clear recognition of Purpose, but it is Purpose restricted to the bounds of Nature. In other words, it is Immanent Purpose. It is not above as well as within the cosmic process but wholly within it. But can Purpose be solely immanent? To be immanent must it not also be transcendent? It is the very nature of Purpose to have an end in view. The end may emerge but slowly and by degrees, it may even take on a changed form, but it cannot come *out* of a process purely as its product. It may not be visible as Purpose until the process is well on its way, but when it is recognized it implies some form of transcendence.

There is no reason why the quality of *transcendence* should in any sense impair or limit *immanence*. In fact it is necessary to it. The time may come when Transcendence-Immanence will be hyphenated, as Space-Time has been. Purpose is an activity of Mind, and Mind cannot be other than both transcendent and immanent. That is its nature. It goes out of itself into that which is other and yet does not lose itself in the other. Transcendence-Immanence is as essential in philosophy as Space-Time in physics. If the universe reveals Purpose, it reveals Mind, and if the issue of Purpose is in any sense *good*, it reveals *Good Mind, i.e.,* Divine Fatherhood. In other words, one is carried back to the Logos.[9]

But this is to anticipate our inquiry. We are at the beginning not the end of our journey. Our present inquiry is: Can the Fatherhood of God be interpreted in a sufficiently reasonable as well as religious way to ap-

[9] Nothing could be more strikingly, though unintentionally, interpretative and corroborative of the Logos conception than Professor Whitehead's "Principle of Concretion." Cf. *Religion in the Making* and Dr. Wieman's *The Wrestle of Religion with Truth,* Chapter XI.

prove itself as not only the purest, highest, and most adequate conception of God possible, but also most in conformity with all known facts? *Can it be shown to be in such harmony with the universe, and with human life, that the unfolding knowledge both of nature and of man not only does not compromise it but actually tends to strengthen and sustain it?* In attempting to find an answer to this question an endeavor will be made to trace briefly the rise and progress of the idea of Divine Fatherhood, to relate it to other ideas and experiences, to encounter some of the obstacles which stand in its way, and to trace its beneficent effects upon human life.

IV

Before entering upon this venturesome task it is well to anticipate a difficulty which arises in the effort to obtain any single, satisfying conception of God; *i.e.,* the difficulty of finding an all-embracing term, whether definitive or descriptive, sufficient to compress within itself the full content of thought and feeling which attaches to the idea of God. The choice is necessarily limited to either a metaphysical or a metaphorical term. Which is the better?

Something is to be said for metaphysical terms for God, *e.g.,* the One, the Infinite, the Absolute, the Eternal. Such designations are free from limiting, anthropomorphic meanings. They elevate the idea above littleness.

They keep faith with the prophet's word: "My thoughts are not your thoughts, neither are your ways my ways, saith the Lord." Yet, on the other hand, they are cold, distant, formal. They stimulate reflection, but fail to stir emotion; they answer for hours of contemplation but not for hours of need. They are inadequate for everyday use. Nor do they suffice for those flood tides of worship and gratitude when the soul desires a conception of God which does not chill but deepens its devotion. In a word, metaphysical conceptions do not answer to the needs of prayer; and prayer is the very soul of religion.

The best conception requires to be one that is both simple and comprehensible, yet also ample and comprehensive, one which will serve all sorts and conditions of men—that will be understood by the child and the peasant, yet will not alienate the thinker and the man of culture—one that will draw all men of all ages and races together in a common faith and fraternity. The nearest to such a conception that can be had, as proved by experience and tested by reason, seems to be the simple name used by Jesus, full of reflective meaning and devout affection, and one that has won an ever widening acceptance—"Our Father which art in Heaven." [10]

[10] "The word Father itself has experienced a change. The attributes of human fatherhood have an ethical quality to-day among Christian peoples which was unknown even to the Jewish home in the days before Christ. Justice, love, care, guidance, education—the common duties of a father to his child as we know them—are largely drawn from Christ's teaching of the worth of each individual soul to the Father." Olive Meacham.

V

The adoption of the name Father does not exclude abstract and metaphysical terms for God. Imaginative and philosophical ideas of God may readily coexist and harmonize.[11] For the mind naturally sees the same object at one time in its abstract, conceptual form and at another time in its imaginative and emotional aspect. How these are related to each other may not be clear, but there is no inherent contradiction between them.

The chief reason why *Father* is the best name for God is that it is a human term deified. Religion is a human-divine experience; it cannot be taken out of the realm of human affections and obligations, hopes and fears, and retain its vitality. The humanness and intimacy of the term Father expose it—it is true—to the liability of being taken literally, thus reducing Isaiah's Holy One "high and lifted up" to the level of an earthly parent.

This has undoubtedly been the effect, if not the teaching, of much modern theology. The idea of a complaisant and easy-going God, too soft-hearted to maintain a moral order, has too far taken the place of that wholesome "fear of the Lord" which is the beginning of wisdom. It is this misconception which gave point to Nietzsche's savage declaration that the Christian God is "one of the most corrupt concepts of God ever arrived at on earth." But this is a complete misunderstanding of the true nature

[11] Cf. J. B. Pratt, *The Religious Consciousness,* pp. 204 ff.

of Fatherhood. Sentimentality has no part in it, although *sentiment* has. Neither the patriarchal ideal of fatherhood, nor the modern implies weakness or complacency. The first article of the Apostles' Creed—still fresh with the vital experience of the early Church—saves the idea of Divine Fatherhood from moral ineptitude by declaring: "I believe in God the *Father Almighty*." Browning's replete line puts the same truth with more of hesitancy but with great suggestiveness:

So the All-Great, were the All-Loving too—

It is the aim of this discussion to present some of the wider aspects of Divine Fatherhood. Its thesis may be briefly restated thus: Progress in the conception of God —philosophical as well as practical—lies not in advancing beyond the idea of God as Father but rather in advancing more deeply *into* it.

CHAPTER II

The Fatherhood of God a Symbol

Divine Fatherhood a Symbol in the form of an Analogy—Jesus' Use and Defense of Symbolism—The Trinity another Type of Symbol and one that has been greatly misunderstood—Opposition from natural Instincts and Motives to a pure and lofty Conception of God; the Reign of Spiritism—Mythology as an Obstacle to Pure Monotheism— Sex Worship, associated with Motherhood, transcended by Judaism and Christianity—The Part played by Individuals in the Climb toward the Ethical Monotheism which prepared the Way for Divine Fatherhood.

I

TO SAVE the conception of God as Father from the danger of degradation to the commonplace it needs only to be remembered that Fatherhood is neither more nor less than a *symbol*. This seems at first a defect, but reflection shows otherwise. For a symbol may be the best possible expression of a spiritual reality. A symbol is that which, by means of some form of association (the word is a Greek compound, meaning *thrown together*), represents something greater than itself.[1] The

---

[1] "A symbol, briefly described, is an object which stands for another object, or is still significant if it stands for no object." R. M. Eaton, *Symbolism and Truth*, p. 21. Needless to say, the use of the term

27

association may be due to a related event, as the cross is the symbol of Christianity because of the crucifixion of Christ; or to some resemblance in appearance or function, as the anchor is a symbol of hope because it holds fast to that which is secure; or it may be an interior analogy (*i.e.*, a likeness in nature) as bread is an analogy of spiritual food because of its nourishing quality. Fatherhood is a symbol by analogy. It associates God with a human father because of a correspondence, however limited, of nature and relationship.

There are various other analogies for God which are full of beauty and meaning. There is, for instance, the imperishable analogue of the Twenty-third Psalm. The Shepherd name for God will never lose its appeal, however far we travel from the pastoral life; yet the image of a Shepherd could not be so universalized as to serve in place of that of a Father.

Analogy affords the best kind of symbolism, because it goes beneath surface suggestions to an inherent likeness in nature. And yet an analogy is only a symbol and should be used as such and nothing more. The danger in the use of Fatherhood as a symbol of God is that the correspondence will be pressed into a complete one, whereas the point of contact, while it is deep and vital, is also limited. The analogy warrants us in regarding God as Father, yet not in limiting Him thereby. In other

---

symbol here is far removed from what Stuart Sherman called "the black bats of the Freudian cave."

words, his Fatherhood transcends, while it embraces—exceeds, while it resembles—human fatherhood.

The spiritual world, by reason of its very nature and relationships, can find adequate expression only in parable, metaphor, symbol—something, that is, which appeals to the imagination. Poetry illustrates the use of symbol at its best. "The fact that poetic form is the only possible one is a sign that we are in the presence of the highest."[2] Religion seizes symbols as a living organism selects its nutriment. Without them it would be barren and speechless.[3] Light, life, the sun, the wind, the rain, sowing, pruning, reaping—such common but meaningful things as these furnish incomparable symbols of the spiritual life.

II

Jesus not only used symbol and parable freely, but recognized the principle involved and explicitly justified it. "And when he was alone, they that were about him with the twelve asked of him the parables. And he said unto them, Unto you is given the mystery of the kingdom of God: but unto them that are without, all things are done in parables: that seeing they may see, and not perceive; and hearing they may hear, and not understand;

[2] Höffding, *Philosophy of Religion*, p. 207.
[3] "Christendom applies the term Father to God because Jesus did so; furthermore Jesus did so because 'father' was in his time the best symbol that human language could offer to denominate THAT SOMETHING which is beyond comprehension and appellation." Alberto Rembao.

lest haply they should turn again, and it should be for-
given them. And he saith unto them, Know ye not this
parable? and how shall ye know all the parables?" [4]
The parable, or symbol, at once invites the open mind
and baffles the closed mind. "That seeing they may see,
and not perceive; and hearing they may hear, and not
understand." "He that hath ears to hear, let him hear."
Jesus did not mean by such words, I take it, to thrust
aside the dull mind as incompetent for spiritual truth;
but rather to arouse it, as could be done in no other way.
The mind that he meant to balk and rebuke by the use
of parable is the self-satisfied mind which thinks it knows
all that is to be known, when its knowledge is merely
external.

What a world of symbols is this! Everything means
more than its outward seeming. There are "underlying
analogies, secret subterranean passages between matter
and soul, chromatic scales, whereat we dimly guess, by
which the Almighty modulates through all the keys of
creation." [5] There is a Logos in all things, an inner
signification which leads the mind onward, inward to
spiritual meanings and values. To miss these is to gain
the whole world and lose its Soul.[6]

It is thus with the symbol of Fatherhood. It means
more than it says. It seizes a mystical human relationship and purifies it, exalts it, recreates it, carries it on

---

[4] Mark 4:10-13.   [5] Francis Thompson, *Shelley*.
[6] In the spiritual (personal) realm even the common prepositions like
"in" and "above" lose their literal meaning and symbolize personal
relationships.

into a wealth and fullness which transfigures the human relationship itself. "Religion," writes one of the philosophical scientists of our time, "is the vision of something which stands beyond, behind and within, the passing flux of immediate things, something which is real, and yet waiting to be realized, something which is a remote possibility, and yet the greatest of present facts, something which gives meaning to all that passes, and yet eludes apprehension, something whose possession is the first good, and yet is beyond all reach; something which is the ultimate ideal, and the hopeless quest." [7] As Sabatier has said, "The world is ruled by symbol, not by science." "He who has overlooked the tremendous emotional power of the symbolic expression of a religious truth has failed to understand much of the hold that religion has over a very large number of men and women." [8]

Is the term Father, then, adequate for those deep and wide as well as intimate meanings which the thought of God requires?   Has it spiritual dimensions sufficient to provide motive and reason for the existence of a universe, for the understanding of humanity and its history, and at the same time to retain warmth and personal quality sufficient to relate the individual directly and simply to God—in a word, to satisfy both mind and heart?   No—we may venture to answer in anticipation of the result of our discussion—if it be narrowly, half-literally, and inadequately conceived.   Yes, if it be under-

[7] A. N. Whitehead, "Religion and Science," *Atlantic Monthly,* August, 1923.

[8] James B. Pratt, *The Religious Consciousness,* p. 206.

stood expansively, symbolically, sympathetically. Indeed, as has been already maintained and as we hope to make more clear, no other conception, religious, scientific or philosophical, is comprehensive enough, vital enough, true enough to experience as a whole, to interpret God in His relation both to human life and to the universe.

III

There is another Christian symbol for God into which theology has sought to compress the metaphysical conception of God—*i.e.*, the Trinity. It is a symbol of quite another kind from that of Fatherhood, yet one which—in spite of the fact that it has been persistently misunderstood—is full of meaning.

A numerical symbol applied to Personality is at once inadequate and at the same time full of suggestion. Trinity is probably the best intellectual symbol of God possible. The reason for this is that it stands for certain essential characteristics of Perfect Personality: (1) Self-differentiation; (2) Completeness; (3) Unity.

Finite personality itself is an imperfect trinity. Every personality, as such, is both transcendent and immanent and yet retains its identity. The Infinite Personality, to be personal, must be of the same nature as our own—only in completeness. Threeness symbolizes Completeness as well as Self-subsistence. "Number vanishes," as Augustine said, or serves only as symbol.

[Handwritten marginal note:] This is very weak! In comparison to the orthodox – Trinity – is divine! – in calling God – Triune in the same Brown is unwilling in calling God – personality (Father) – perfect personality i.e. Christ – & indwelling Spirit or H.S. Creative Purpose

The absurdity of "three persons in One"—which crept
into the doctrine, but which one may search for in vain
in the Nicene Creed—has so perverted the doctrine of the
Trinity as to almost completely obscure its real meaning
and value. Rightly understood, it is the most adequate
philosophical conception of God achieved by human
thought. *At the same time Trinity is inferior and subordinate to Fatherhood as a symbol of God.* Unless it
helps to a larger understanding of God as Father, it is
worse than worthless—but as a help to such an understanding it is of great value.

IV

Returning to Fatherhood as assumptively the purest
and best symbol of God, the student of religion will not
fail to recognize that, simple as it is and early as its lineaments appeared in racial religious experience, it was
only after prolonged spiritual growth and severe opposition that such a conception could assume a controlling
place in human thought, expelling the hordes of lower
and contradictory ideas which disputed its advance.

It is difficult for us, at our advanced stage in the development of religion, to realize the obstacles against
which progress in the direction of intellectual clarity and
spiritual and moral purity in the idea of God had to contend. It will be instructive to dwell for a little upon
some of these backward tendencies, for in this way we
shall be enabled to realize more fully how slowly and

with what difficulty belief in the Fatherhood of God, simple as it now seems to us, established itself.

Nothing is more characteristic of religion in its lower stages than belief in spirits. Earth and air were peopled with these creations, for the preliterate and prescientific mind—a most unhappy by-product of the religious sentiment. For the spirits seem, as a rule, to have been regarded as malevolent, unless propitiated.[9] Hence came fear, as paralyzing and exhausting as it was groundless and gratuitous. How great a curse the belief in evil spirits has been, what a weight it has hung about the neck of humanity, what senseless and extravagant forms it has assumed, how it may linger on in the face of a comparatively advanced culture, may be clearly seen in the case of China, when spirits of the dead and nature spirits have so long thronged earth and air, disputing human mastery at every point. Nor has China been exceptional in this regard.

The long reign of spiritism in religion makes a dark and distressing chapter in the life of humanity; and the tragedy of it is, that, as Paul asserts, it appears to have been, due in the main, to "vain reasoning"—the creation of a populous realm of malevolence out of nothing. It would be pharasaic to condemn the primitive mind for conjuring up this enemy to its own peace and progress; but neither can it be absolved from blame.[10]

[9] "Generally speaking, a spirit is regarded, unless properly propitiated, as malevolent or maleficent more often than as benevolent and beneficent." Hastings' Dictionary of Religion and Ethics, vol. III, p. 566.
[10] This does not mean that *Animism* as a whole is a corruption of religion. It was quite natural for the child-man to think of all things

That the savage himself was able to realize how false
and disastrous the tyranny of spiritism, in the form of
tabus, may become is evidenced in the striking act of the
Hawaiian people in abolishing their *tabu* system just before the arrival of the American missionaries in 1820.
As a rule, however, the reign of spiritism seems not to
have been broken until some higher religion has come in
to reveal its folly and to offer something better to sup-
plant it.

V

Mythology is another religious phenomenon which
stood in the path of the ethical monotheism which prepared the way for Divine Fatherhood. The myth-
ological impulse itself is by no means unnatural or
sinister. The imagination of child-races naturally tends
to exercise itself in weaving fanciful tales concerning the
origin of the world and of man and in accounting for
strange phenomena in nature. In these myths the gods
naturally play a prominent part. Many myths, notably
among the Scandinavian peoples and the American In-
dians, are full of poetry and pristine reverence.

Yet when one looks, even cursorily, into the maelstrom

---

as having life like himself. (Cf. George W. Gilmore, *Animism.*) But
this *Animatism,* as it has been termed, should be distinguished from
belief in spirits. It is difficult to see why imagination should have taken
the direction of peopling earth, air, and sky with spirits, so malevolent
and harmful, without some more or less willful misuse of intellect and
imagination, for which backward peoples have had to pay the heavy
price of self-imposed misery and delayed development.

of race mythology, it becomes evident how large a number of myths are puerile, unsocial, and degrading, indicating a misdirection of the imagination as well as of the religious sentiment. This appears quite clearly in the case of so gifted and highly developed a people as the Greeks, whose mythology, along with much that is beautiful and poetic, is filled with stories of the gods and goddesses which Plato naturally judged unfit to be employed in the education of youth.[11]   The creation myths of Japan furnish a striking illustration of the indiscriminate blending of fancies pure and fancies foul, of the charming and the grotesque, the moral and the immoral in mythology. Magic, necromancy, divination, witchcraft, are forms of "vain reasoning" which produced various abnormalities, including the professional practitioner who, himself deluded, deluded others, until life was dominated by all sorts of terrifying beliefs and hateful practices.

These by-products of religion, in which unrestrained imagination blended with false thinking to produce a hideous incubus upon the soul of man, are foreign to its true nature and may be regarded as divergencies from the normal pathway of development. The same may be said of some aspects of totemism, theriolatry, and the rites of initiation into the tribal life, although each of these, especially the latter, served the ends of tribal and national solidarity.[12]

[11] "Those, said I, which Hesiod and Homer tell us, and the other poets, for they composed false fables to mankind." *The Republic,* Book II.

[12] The theory of the Durkheim School adopted by many students of religion in America, that religion is to be understood as merely an

VI

In hallowing and controlling the sex instinct, morality, in alliance with the purer type of religion, has had one of its most severe and prolonged struggles.[13] The Old Testament makes it quite clear that the temptation to sexualize religion, which was so widespread, through its supposed association with the fertility of the fields, constituted a large factor in the degrading influences which Israel felt pressing in from the foreign religions about her and before which she continually fell.[14]

In this worship of the fertility principle in nature the Semitic races, and others, associated the female deity oftener than the male deity with the principle of fecundity.[15] Throughout Europe and Asia Minor the leading cult was that of *Mater Magna,* or her counterparts, Hera, Cybele, and Artemis. It was a well-founded instinct of hostility which led the priests of the magnificent temple of Artemis in Ephesus to set the town in uproar against

idealization of the social bond, finds much in all the forms of undeveloped religion to support it; but there is much also that this theory of the function of religion fails to account for.

[13] It would be unjust to condemn as pure perversion the sex symbolism which is so prominent in primitive and undeveloped religion. The sense of sacredness attached to sex was a far greater honor to humanity than the degradation and commercialization of it of which civilization has been guilty.

[14] Upon this phase of religion, Frazer's *The Golden Bough* furnishes more than ample information.

[15] See the article "Baal," by William Robertson Smith, in the Encyclopædia Britannica; also Washburn, *Origin and Evolution of Religion,* pp. 276 ff.

the preaching of Paul with the cry, "Great is Diana of the Ephesians!" Great indeed was the hold of the cult of Nature worship, celebrated as the *Artemisium,* upon the life not only of Asia Minor but of Rome herself, which was threatened by the severe purity of the Christ cult.[16]

When, therefore, the question arises, as it sometimes does, Why choose fatherhood for the symbol of God, rather than motherhood? the answer cannot be detached from the history of religion. While the Christian mother has as much, if not more, than the father, of those loving and protective qualities which Christianity conceives as belonging to God, still, in the history of religion the idea of fatherhood has been freer from sex implications than has that of motherhood.

It needed Christianity with its lofty vision of the Virgin Mother, to rescue womanhood from a lower to a higher religious meaning. It is an incident of dramatic significance that the Council of Ephesus (431 A.D.), which condemned Nestorius and sanctioned the extravagant and superstitious title given to Mary, "Mother of God," was held in the city where religion had so long consecrated the naturalistic aspect of womanhood rather than its pure, holy, and loving character. The cult of

[16] "The commonest conception through the Mediterranean world, including Greece, Asia Minor, Syria, and even Babylonia, regarded the earth—or the soil of the local fields—as a mother or fruitful wife, closely connected with some Youth, son or brother or consort, who represented, in varying proportions, the Sun or Spring or Year." Gilbert Murray, "Pagan Religion at the Coming of Christianity," in A. S. Peake's *New Testament Commentary,* pp. 629 ff.

the Virgin, in spite of its superstition and incongruity, did much to win for woman the recognition of her purer and nobler qualities. Yet it would have created wide misunderstanding to have made motherhood, instead of fatherhood, the Christian symbol of God.

Many and strong were the tendencies in the development of religious experience which led away from the idea of God as Father. Strait was the gate and narrow the way that led toward it, and long and difficult was the journey. "The whole story of the development of monotheism and the growth of the moral conception of the deity has been largely determined by a kind of implicit logic, a sense of dissatisfaction with the incongruous." [17] This implicit logic had to contend against an explicit temptation to degrade and sensualize the religious sentiment. While "the monotheistic idea was at most periods in the air," [18] before it could become a reality in human faith and life a long and severe struggle against misconceptions and downward tendencies was necessary.

VII

The part played by individuals in this Godward climb seems to have been large. Outstanding individuals, superior intellectually and morally, and peculiarly sensitive to spiritual influences, although often ignored and repulsed by their fellows, have exercised a wider influence than

[17] J. B. Pratt, *The Religious Consciousness,* p. 204.
[18] Article "Religion," Encyclopaedia Britannica, p. 62.

they themselves could realize. A few of these, like Ahkenaton, Zarathustra, Confucius, Abraham, Moses, and the prophets of Israel, have left their names to be honored by succeeding generations; but most are forgotten, although the influence of their Godward aspiration has entered into the moral and spiritual progress of the race. One may find a picturesque example of the humbler among these finer souls—a kind of Unknown Soldier, so to speak, in the great campaign for religious progress—in the old Amerind whom Francis Parkman describes in *The Oregon Trail:*

. . . After advancing for some time, I conceived myself to be entirely alone; but coming to a part of the glen in a great measure free of trees and undergrowth, I saw at some distance the black head and red shoulders of an Indian among the bushes above. The reader need not prepare himself for a startling adventure, for I have none to relate. The head and shoulders belonged to Mene-Seela, my best friend in the village. As I had approached noiselessly with my moccasined feet, the old man was quite unconscious of my presence; and turning to a point where I could gain an unobstructed view of him, I saw him seated alone, immovable as a statue, among the rocks and trees. His face was turned upward, and his eyes seemed riveted on a pine-tree springing from a cleft in the precipice above. The crest of the pine was swaying to and fro in the wind, and its long limbs waved slowly up and down, as if the tree had life. Looking for a while at the old man, I was satisfied that he was engaged in an act of worship, or prayer, or communion of some kind with a supernatural being. I longed to penetrate his thoughts, but I could do nothing more than conjecture and speculate. I knew that though the intellect of an Indian can embrace the idea of an all-wise, all-powerful

Spirit, the supreme Ruler of the universe, yet his mind will not always ascend into communion with a being that seems to him so vast, remote, and incomprehensible; and when danger threatens, when his hopes are broken, and trouble overshadows him, he is prone to turn for relief to some inferior agency, less removed from the ordinary scope of his faculties.

It is difficult to conceive of the gradual uplift of mind and spirit toward a Supreme Being, on the part of many races and individuals, against the downward drag of lower influences as other than a response to One who "in divers portions and in divers manners" has been imparting Himself in all ages and lands to those capable and willing to receive Him. The climb toward Ethical Monotheism is thus seen as also a drawing of men to God through revelation of Himself to them. Thus arduously was the way won for the supreme disclosure of the Father through the Son.

CHAPTER III

Fatherhood Revealed Through Sonship

Foregleams of Divine Fatherhood in both preliterate and higher Religions—Jesus' intense Realization of God as Spiritual Father of all men makes him virtually the Discoverer of this Truth—His Prayer for Harmony in the two-fold Realm of God—His Teaching of God as the Father of Nature, as well as of Men, and caring for both according to the Principle of Comparative Worth—The Sparrow's Fall, the Lost Sheep and the Prodigal Son as Insights into the Character and Method of Divine Love—Universal Fatherhood as difficult and as reasonable a Faith in Jesus' Time as in ours—The Fatherhood of God not obscured by Paul and the Author of the Fourth Gospel, but enriched and amplified.

JESUS was not the first to call God Father. The religious traditions and literatures of many peoples show foregleams of the same homely yet exalted idea of God emerging more and more clearly from the religious consciousness.

I

The dim foreshadowing of an idea of God having something at least of the character of Fatherhood begins to reveal itself in what may be termed the Prototheism of

42

primitive religion, *i.e.*, the indistinct discernment of a lofty Moral Being, too remote to take part in human affairs and too good to need worship.[1] In the more advanced religions the idea of a Fatherly God becomes constantly clearer and more meaningful. In a Babylonian hymn (*c.* 2000 B.C.) *Marduk* is addressed thus: "Lord art thou, and like a father and a mother."[2] In an Egyptian hymn (*c.* 1700 B.C.) *Amen Ra* is called:

> "Lord of truth, father of the gods,
> Maker of men, creator of the animals."

The use by the Greeks of the term for Zeus "Father of gods and men," is forward-looking, and at times in their literature he exhibits truly fatherly attributes, as in many passages in Homer and in the well-known hymn to Zeus in Æschylus.

Such foreshadowings of Divine Fatherhood are meaningful, though limited in scope. In most cases, alongside the Father-God there are lesser gods who share his rule. Along with beneficent and fatherly attributes there are also traits and qualities which belie them, displaying moral and intellectual defects which make the idea of Divine Fatherhood little more than "a gleam in darkness" —prophetic but not determinative.

A far higher conception of Divine Fatherhood appears

---

[1] See: Andrew Lang, *The Making of Religion;* F. B. Jevons, *Introduction to the History of Religion;* Le Roy, *The Religion of the Primitives;* D. G. Brinton, *Religion of Primitive Peoples.*

[2] This and the hymn immediately following may be found in the admirable anthology of Caroline M. Hill: *The World's Great Religious Poetry.*

in the Old Testament. The Hebrew prophets and psalmists attained a lofty ethical conception of God as a Father. Although He was generally conceived as Father of His people as a whole, rather than of individuals, occasionally a devout spirit rose to a more intimate, personal conception, as when the psalmist cried: "Like as a father pitieth his children, so the Lord pitieth them that fear him." [3]

II

When we turn from these foregleams of Fatherhood to the faith of Jesus, we have passed from twilight to full day. Here the conception of God as a true Father becomes a living reality. "The procedure of taking the consequences seriously," writes Professor Whitehead, "marks the real discovery of a theory." [4] Jesus took the Fatherhood of God seriously, and because it meant everything to him it came to mean so much to others.

Jesus' characteristic designation for God is reported about 150 times in the four Gospels to be "Father," used in various connections.

"The Father," used in sixty-one verses.

"O Father," in prayer to God—seventeen verses.

"My Father," in fifty verses.

"Your Father," sometimes "your heavenly Father," in eighteen verses.

[3] Ps. 103:13.
[4] A. N. Whitehead, *The Concept of Nature*, p. 26.

"Our Father," in the Lord's prayer. (Matthew 6 : 9; Luke 11:2.)

Altogether the word "Father" as referring to God occurs about 300 times in the New Testament.

Nowhere among the sacred scriptures of the world is there to be found even an approximation to this wide and consistent usage among all writers of the sacred scriptures of Christianity of this simple, vital, intimate, feelingful, personal name, "Father," used along with the more abstract term "God." [5]

It is not the priority of Jesus' teaching of Fatherhood that makes it so significant, but its intense realism. Priority counts for little in such a matter as this, compared to a living and confident realization and the power to convey this realization to others. It was in this that Jesus was creatively original. Upon his lips *Abba* meant more than any name for God ever meant before. So purely and ardently did it issue from the depths of his own experience as to communicate itself to his disciples and through them to others in such vivid reality as to make a new and transforming epoch in the life of the human spirit. This is originality. By this token Divine Fatherhood may be rightly regarded as a discovery, and Jesus as the discoverer.

III

When we look somewhat more closely into the meaning of the Divine Fatherhood to Jesus, we find it characterized by several distinguishing marks. God as Pure Spirit,

[5] Robert E. Hume, *The World's Living Religions,* p. 251.

dwelling in the realm of spirit—such is Jesus' conception. The phrase in the petition for the coming of the Kingdom, "as in heaven so on earth," indicates that Jesus thought of God's realm as twofold. In the one His will reigns supreme, in the other there is discord, which it is the part of all good men to help to overcome in order to secure universal harmony.

How and why this disharmony arose, Jesus does not undertake to explain, further than to attribute it to an Evil Power ("the Evil") from which men are to pray to be delivered. To assume that Jesus necessarily regarded the Evil Power as a Person is quite unwarranted. It is true that he often refers to Satan in the customary language of his day; but that signifies far less than the fact that he once addressed *Peter* as Satan. It will not do to take his words too literally, either as regards Satan or Peter.

In the only reported word of his in which Jesus faces thoughtfully the question of the nature of evil he attributes its origin to the human heart. "For from within, out of the heart of men, evil thoughts proceed, fornications, thefts, murders, adulteries, covetings, wickednesses, deceit, lasciviousness, an evil eye, railing, pride, foolishness: all these evil things proceed from within, and defile the man." [6] This, for Jesus, is not a world divided between God and Satan. It is God's world, in which evil is an intrusion, a very real and awful power but one whose reign is coming to an end.[7]

[6] Mark 7:21-23.   [7] Luke 10:18.

IV

The Father of men was for Jesus—although in a some-what different sense—also the Father of the natural world. This is implicit, but real in his teaching. It appears, *e.g.*, in his reference to the birds and flowers in the Sermon on the Mount and in his joyous exclamation: "I thank Thee, Father, *Lord of Heaven and Earth!*" These sayings would indicate that God the Father, in Jesus' mind, is not only Creator and Sustainer of men and of all creatures, but their Guardian.[8]

This care, although Jesus thinks of it as extending to the whole animate creation, by virtue of the principle of comparative worth he conceives as far more intimately concerned with human beings than with other creatures. Men are of more value than many sparrows, and beside human beings sheep are—sheep. Still more closely is the Divine Oversight, in Jesus' mind, concerned with those who are the chosen builders of the Kingdom. Of them he uses that arresting hyperbole, "Even the very hairs of your heads are all numbered."

Here is a conception of Divine Care based upon inherent degrees of worth as well as upon capacity and commission for service. It is impartial, but not indiscriminate; all-inclusive, but not all-confusing. The principle

[8] "No other religious teacher of mankind speaks so lovingly of Nature. Whether he refers to her order . . . her mystery . . . or her restfulness and freedom from care . . . He saw in all these varying aspects a revelation of the goodness of God." J. G. Simpson, *Landmarks in the Struggle between Science and Religion,* p. 259.

commends itself as clear and just. "If man is spiritual and the stars are not, then God is vastly more concerned about the selfishness of a child than about the wreck of a solar system," [9] writes Bishop Temple, in another bold, but not unwarranted, hyperbole.

V

Jesus viewed the world in the freshness and purity of the spiritual dawn that suffused his soul and in the unembarrassed intrepidity of an unscientific age. Can we, under the blazing noon of modern science, history, and philosophy, look upon our vastly expanded cosmos through his eyes and see it as all pervaded and illuminated with the Divine Presence and Care? At first thought it seems impossible. Science has taught us much since Jesus' day. Yet it is by no means certain that it is with wiser, because more scientific, eyes that we of to-day survey our wider universe. If, after passing through the skepticism begotten by enlarged knowledge, we were to attain once more to the simplicity of faith, perhaps we should be nearer to the heart of reality than we now are—our knowledge transfused with a deeper wisdom.

With all the joyousness and hopefulness of his outlook upon nature, Jesus did not close his eyes to its darker side. Witness his word concerning the fall of the sparrow. Within that tender saying lies deep reflection, as

[9] William Temple, *Christ the Truth*, p. 115.

well as clear-eyed observation. "Are not two sparrows sold for a farthing? and not one of them shall fall on the ground without your Father." [10] The restraint of these words is as significant as their confidence. Jesus does not say that it is by the Father's ordering that the sparrow falls, nor that He sorrows over it as something which He cannot prevent. He simply affirms that the sparrow's fall comes within the Father's ken. His penetrative insight perceived in it something more than the mere incident itself. Viewed in the light of an all-embracing Love, he saw in so apparently trivial an event a deeper meaning.

Tennyson's well-known lines express a similar, if more tentative, faith:

> That not a worm is cloven in vain,
> That not a moth, with vain desire
> Is shrivelled in a fruitless fire,
> Or but subserves another's gain.

Is there a key here to the sparrow's fall? Did Jesus see each least life so linked to the whole that under the Divine guidance even its undoing issues in good to all, including the one that suffers? Perhaps, but all that he said was simply: *God cares*.

Divine Fatherhood was to Jesus a Fatherhood of Love, especially toward men, a love not merely benevolent and kind, but sorrowing, searching, sacrificial—a love like that of the Good Shepherd seeking the sheep that is lost, like that of the yearning father waiting for the prodigal's return. The different ways in which love acts in these

[10] Matt. 10:29.

two parables is significant. Both are full of affection. The shepherding love goes in search of the wanderer (and that is sometimes the fatherly way), but still more fatherly is the love that waits at home, knowing well that self-will is best won by no urgency of following but rather by patient waiting upon the issues of experience and reflection. Here is the heart of Fatherliness—inviting, but not compelling, reconciliation, love, communion.

VI

Finally, the Divine Fatherhood, as Jesus conceived and taught it, is *universal*. His environment and training did not conduce to such a faith as this. Son of an exclusive race, wrapped in its own traditions and history, living under the heel of a foreign power, Jesus was naturally chiefly concerned for his own suffering and aspiring people. The lost sheep of the house of Israel—were not these enough to engage his whole thought and concern? Yet not to them could the breadth and outreach of his sympathy be confined. Upon the multitudes "he had compassion." The publican, the Samaritan, the centurion, the Syrophenician woman—these won his unaffected solicitude. They, too, were the children of the Father.

Whoever has the courage to accept and act upon faith in God as the Universal Father has Jesus as his comrade and leader in the great adventure. Whoever finds this too good to be true must, in this regard at least, part with Jesus as a trustworthy interpreter of the religious consciousness.

It is plausible to discount Jesus' faith in God in view of the fact that his world was so circumscribed and provincial as compared with ours. It was comparatively easy, it may be said, for a sanguine Galilean of the first century, with his limited outlook and knowledge, to think of God as Father, but to-day it is quite another matter, with the bounds of the universe so extended, the avenues into the past leading backward and downward into primeval shadows, with the problems raised by philosophy so complex and difficult, the facts disclosed by anthropology, sociology, economics, psychology, so confusing and so conducive to quite other interpretations than his.

And yet, when one stops to consider the situation, was there not as much to challenge belief in God as Father in Jesus' day as in ours? His people, whom he had been taught to regard as very dear to God, were under the yoke of a world-power that gave them no opportunity to fulfill their mission to the world. About him were misery, disease, insanity, hypocrisy, hopelessness, the religion of the leaders of his people hardened into Pharisaic formalism, the people themselves dull, materialistic, sign-seeking. Evidently Jesus had noted well all the apparent contradictions to God's Fatherhood about him—the fall of the sparrow, the wanton destruction of the earthquake, the ravages of flood and storm, the hard inhumanity and self-righteousness of the leaders of religion, the confused helplessness of the people, who were "as sheep having no shepherd." These things were before him in all their brutal reality. He did not turn away, nor close his eyes to them. He witnessed his Father's house profaned, His will disobeyed, his own message misconceived, himself rejected. What was there to sustain the faith that the world about him was God's world, his people God's people and He their Heavenly Father, yes, the Father of all men? Little, save a sublime faith, a deep consciousness of sonship, an insight that looked beneath the surface to profounder realities, a trust that never wavered, whatever outward contradictions might arise.

There is as little to-day as then to arouse and sustain faith in the Fatherhood of God and—as much. Only faith itself can create this confidence. Now, as then, it is only the filial attitude that can find adequate assurance of the Divine Fatherhood. *This attitude Jesus awakens in his followers.*

VII

There is to-day a widespread idea that the simple "religion of Jesus"—his clear ethical teachings and his faith in a Father-God—was transformed by Paul into a cumbersome mystical and doctrinal "religion about Jesus" in which the Fatherhood of God was obscured, pushed into the background of a Christocentric Christianity. It is a serious misconception. On the contrary, the truth of Divine Fatherhood was enriched, expanded, completed, by having incorporated into it the personality of him who revealed the Father as no other has ever done. As "the God and Father of our Lord Jesus Christ," He is seen to be, a hundredfold more clearly and fully, the God and Father of every Christian and of all mankind.

If to magnify Christ means to minimize God, Paul was certainly guilty; for he greatly magnified and exalted Christ. Yet his Christ is not a rival of God but the Revealer of the Father who, instead of withdrawing honor from Him, is conceived as delivering "up the kingdom to God, even the Father . . . that God may be all in all," [11] and to confess whom is "to the glory of God the Father." [12] To find in Paul's Christ one who is in any sense a substitute or rival of God the Father, and not His Son and Servant and Revealer, is to quite misread the apostle's whole meaning and intention. The entire purpose and effect of the Christology of Paul was not to diminish but to exalt God the Father, without Whom the Son could mean nothing.

The Fourth Gospel, that book of profound spiritual insight, corresponds to and carries on the Christology of Paul. The author finds the Fatherhood of God—unveiled as it is by the Eternal Christ—a rich and moving truth. The key word of the Johannine Gospel may be said to be: "He that hath seen me hath seen the Father." Christ constantly subordinates himself to the Father. "I came not to do mine own will but the will of him that sent me." Here is the counterpart of Paul's "who being in

[11] I Cor. 15:24, 28.
[12] Phil. 2:11.

the form of God, thought not equality with God a thing to be grasped at, but humbled himself."

The Fatherhood of God, as depicted in the Synoptic Gospels, instead of losing anything of its human touch, or of its distinctness and reality, by being expanded by Paul and the author of the Johannine Gospel into universal human and cosmic relationships, gains in warmth as well as radiance, just as the rising sun passing into the full splendor of midday diffuses more of its life-giving resources.

CHAPTER IV

Divine Fatherhood vs. Perfect Personality

Perfect Personality, the philosophical Counterpart of God the Father, an Abstraction which supplements but does not surpass the Symbol of Fatherhood—The Concept of Perfect Personality lifts God infinitely above Man yet relates Him intimately to Man—The Perfect Person essentially Creative, finite Persons subcreative—Creation conceivably an imaginative as well as a rational Process—Perfect Personality the distinctly Christian Conception of God when interpreted philosophically.

I

DIVINE Fatherhood translated into philosophic language reads, *Perfect Personality*. This version of Supreme Reality is an illumination, but not an advance; an interpretation, but not a substitution. Personality is implicit in the term Father, as that is implicit in the religious experience as such. Its emergence sheds light on the meaning of Fatherhood but does not supersede it. Personality as a concept is not superior to Fatherhood for the reason that an abstraction is not in itself superior to a symbol. An abstraction has at once the advantage and the defect of its quality. Its advantage is for thought, its defect is for feeling and imagination.

55

To recognize *personality* as an abstraction, however, is not to disparage it. Abstraction is an essential office of thought. The mind is constantly using it, as the number of abstract nouns in constant use testifies. The harm comes only when abstractions are substituted for concrete realities. That way lies, not madness, but meagerness, not error, but defect. There is a form of Idealism which seems to honor the mind by making abstraction the dominating method of reaching reality but which ends in a barren intellectualism, "sicklied o'er with the pale cast of thought." Such a system cannot maintain itself thus encumbered. It reaches its climax in Hegelianism, which loses *personality* in *thought* and which undermines its otherwise superb structure—affronting the mind as well as the heart—by elevating philosophy above religion and then patronizing religion as serving undeveloped minds in lieu of philosophy. That is pure assumption, academic snobbery, an idol of the cave, that will not endure the light of experience and reflection.

This is not to say, however, that abstraction has not a very valuable office to fulfill. To abstract the quality of rationality from a philosopher, goodness from a good man, love from a lover, helps to get nearer to the characteristic traits of each. Yet when these abstractions are detached and regarded apart from those who possess them, they fade and shrivel like leaves torn from a tree. What is needed is not to abstract *from*, but to penetrate *into*, concrete realities by means of abstraction. The only desirable form of detachment is to detach qualities, not from their possessors but from incidental qualities which obscure them, and thus to focus them in their true light. Such abstraction greatly assists the task of interpretation. Thus when John Doe is regarded only as a commonplace individual, among millions of others, he has no especial significance, but when his real though inconspicuous goodness is abstracted from his dullness and mediocrity and he is thus recognized as a good man, his real worth begins to appear. To regard God merely as *Being* is to have a meager and indistinct thought of Him, while to abstract the quality of Personality and recognize Him as the Perfect Person results in a heightened realization of His nature.

There are abstractions and abstractions. Personality is, so to speak, a *synthesis* of abstractions. It first distinguishes and then unites qualities such as self-consciousness, self-identity, freedom, self-direction, worth, holding them in harmonious relation as together belonging to a moral person and supremely to One who is metaphysically, morally, and spiritually perfect. William Blake's tender lines translate abstractions into concrete realities.

> For Mercy, Pity, Peace, and Love,
>   Is God our Father dear;
> And Mercy, Pity, Peace, and Love,
>   Is man, His child and care.

II

The value of the idea of God as Perfect Personality greatens the more one considers it, both in the richness of its inclusions and in the pertinence of its exclusions. It elevates God above the impersonality of the external world, thus showing its superiority to Pantheism, which fails to do this, dragging spiritual and moral qualities down to the level of lower forms of being. At the same time, while it prevents confusing God with the world, Personality suggests and clarifies His immanence within it. For by its very nature personality is both transcendent and immanent. It exists in itself and at the same time goes forth from itself into that which is other than itself. This is as true of human as of Divine personality.

Best of all, the concept *personality* clarifies and conserves the kinship of God and man, while at the same time defining and differentiating them. Human beings are individual selves. Individuality is their hall-mark, their badge, their priesthood. They have self-consciousness, self-identity, unity, memory, and, greatest of all, *moral potentiality*, the capacity to become true persons, *i.e.*, possessors of moral worth and freedom. Personality for human beings is a development, to be won by moral exertion and spiritual culture. They are actuated by a sense of obligation and drawn upward by an ideal and are, therefore, free. This ideal greatens as the individual develops, but in the end gets its meaning from the reality of the Perfect Himself.

As Pure Person, God is not, cannot be, an individual.[1] An individual is a unit, one of a family or a class, having marks which distinguish him, however slightly, from every other, yet having the very ground of his individuality in being one of a kind. It cannot be thus with God. As Pure Person, or Spirit, He is the only one of His kind. Above all, He is yet related to all. He is, as Isaiah saw Him in his vision, high and lifted up, yet His train fills the temple. This is where the polytheist fell short of the true conception of God. To him there was not God, but gods, a group, a family, a class. In the Greek Pantheon the gods and goddesses were distinctly individualized— Zeus, Athena, Poseidon, Hephæstus, and the rest. Zeus was given preëminence, yet remained one among others. This conception had to be transcended before monotheism could come in, with its higher intellectual, moral, and spiritual content. God must be Only God, to be God. He must be the One Supreme Person in order to be rationally related to other forms of being. This does not make Him colorless or unknowable. He is not the Pure Being of Absolutism who resolves away into Nothingness. On the contrary He is "The God and Father of our Lord Jesus Christ," the Perfect Person, just because He has such fullness, such completeness, such apotheosis of the quali-

[1] The term *individual* is, of course, susceptible to so exceptional a meaning as that which Bosanquet gives it in calling God the only true Individual, but this is a singular use of the word, unlikely to gain currency.

ties which ennoble human persons as raises Him to the nth power.

There is a singularly mistaken and persistent notion that Perfection means static passivity. Nothing could be further from the idea itself, or from the teaching of Christian theology. "Icily, regularly, splendidly null" may represent perfection in the realm of forms—although in fact it is at a long remove from the highest beauty—but in the realm of personality perfection means, not the absence of activity but the completeness of it. *The highest activity is not that of striving, developing, achieving; but of outgoing, imparting, creating, sustaining.* This is true even of human personality.

Active Benevolence has always been the essential characteristic of God in Christian doctrine. Such is the teaching of Jesus as well as of Paul, Augustine, Aquinas, and Dante. "My Father worketh hitherto." It is the real essence of Trinitarianism. God is conceived as complete, ceaseless, overflowing Goodness. He creates, not because He desires self-realization but because His nature is Love, Self-impartion.

III

The concept of Perfect Personality throws light also upon the meaning of *creation*. Personality by its very nature is creative. All persons create. It is the nature of self-activity to express itself, to embody itself in form.

Human persons create according to their capacity and

character. Some of their productions are good, true, beautiful; others evil, false, ugly. They are of astonishing variety and degrees of worth or unworth, from poems to factories, from intangible thought-constructs to skyscrapers, from poisonous gases to philosophic systems, from fortresses to air castles.

Yet wonderful as is this creative gift and its resultants, it is all *subcreation*. All of its constructions are secondary, fashioned out of creative material already at hand. The material out of which man creates is all given him. He begins with what already exists; and the worthier his creation the more certain he is that it is only partially his own. When one creates something really good and true —an immortal work of art, an enduring piece of literature, a social institution—or makes a great scientific discovery, he seldom fails to testify that he is conscious that it is not his alone, or even chiefly his, but that the inspiration has come to him from some invisible Source other than himself.

If finite personality is creative, much more so Infinite Personality. If humans can create a bridge, a cathedral, a telephone, a political system, a *Divina Commedia,* a *Hamlet,* a *Sistine Madonna,* a symphony, *pari passu* Divine Personality can create a world, a universe, a system of universes, and, crowning all, a City of God, a Republic of finite persons. → Why a Republic?

This Divine creative activity, while it involves transcendence, is intimately immanental, and that in different forms and degrees. It is immanent in nature, in what ancient philosophy regarded as the union of *form* and *activity* and science calls *force,* and creatively immanent in men personally.

Why then, if the cosmos and all that it contains is the creation of Perfect Personality, has it defects, ill adjustments, discords, imperfections? The answer to this difficulty, as far as it can be divined, would seem to lie in two principles which will be further considered later—freedom and development.

(1) The Creator—so at least one may conceive—imparts out of Himself, as one of His chief gifts, the principle of freedom—inducting it into the universe as part of its being—a freedom which in the lower orders of existence is but an incipient conation or impulse but which increases in scope and intelligence until in man it becomes the power of choice and finally of self-direction.

(2) He creates—so far as we can understand creation —by a process of development, a purposeful procedure toward an augmenting perfection. That this process, as we see it, is developmental, evolutionary, progressive, does not mean that it is necessarily such to the Creator Himself. Physicists are now joining with metaphysicians in regarding change, the "one-way drift" of the cosmos, as not necessarily revealing its essential character from the point of view of an Absolute Mind.

Relativity belongs to the finite mind, not to the Eternal Mind. To the Divine Mind events in a Time Succession may be compresent in an Eternal *Now.* One gets a suggestion of this in the way in which the very word *evolu-*

tion embraces at the moment of its utterance the whole age-long process, still incomplete, which it connotes.

IV

Creative Activity resulting in such a vast, varied, and ever changing universe has been conceived by the human mind in every age as essentially ideational, a thought process, the activity of the Eternal Logos, or Reason. A suggestive enlargement of this conception has lately been proposed by Douglas Fawcett who conceives of creation not so much as a thought process as an *imagining*.

Thus we may come to agree that Divine Imagining is fundamental, that it and its continuing centres furnish the dynamic or 'real dialectic' of creative evolution, that causation, including, of course, all cases of 'physical' happenings, is imaginal process.[2]

Mr. Fawcett thinks that this conception is superior to that of reason, since it provides for an understanding of Time as affording, by means of the principle of *succession,* a field for the Creative Imagining to work in.

This conception of Divine Imagination—or that in God which corresponds to imagination in us—as active in the creative process is illuminating, until it proposes to *substitute* Imagination for Thinking. Imagination without ordered and unified thought would produce a chaos rather than a cosmos. But if to the orderly working of Divine Reason is added the idea of the freedom and wealth of

[2] J. H. Muirhead, *Contemporary British Philosophy,* vol. II, p. 89.

Divine Imagining, producing in connection with the free activity of the organism and of the mind, ever new forms, we have an enriched and perhaps somewhat more adequate conception of the Divine Creative Activity.

V

Just as Divine Fatherhood is *the characteristic Christian conception of God religiously,* so, it may be said, is its counterpart, Perfect Personality, *the characteristic Christian concept philosophically.* Indeed, the concept of personality is itself largely a Christian product and its reference to God the outcome of Christian thought. The judgment of so impartial a historian of philosophy as Dr. Windelband upon this subject may well be quoted:

In opposition to such diabolical subtilizations [as those of the later Neoplatonists, Jamblichus and Proclus], the *development of Christian thought in the Church* preserved its impressive energy by holding fast to the *conception of God as spiritual personality.* It did this, not as the result of philosophical reflection and reasoning, but by virtue of its immediate attachment to the living belief of the Church community, and just in this consisted its psychological strength, its power in the world's history. This faith is breathed in the New Testament; this is defended by all the supporters of patristic theology, and just by this are the limits of the Christian doctrine everywhere defined, as against the Hellenistic solutions of the chief problem in the philosophy of history.

Hellenism sees in personality, in however purely spiritual a manner it may be conceived, a restriction and a characteristic of the finite, which it would keep at a distance from the Supreme Being, and admit only for the particular gods. Christianity, as a living religion, demands a *personal relation of man to the ground of the world conceived of as supreme personality,* and it expresses this demand in the thought of the *divine sonship* of man.

If, therefore, the conception of personality as intrinsic spirituality (*geistiger Innerlichkeit*) expresses the essentially new result, to yield which, theoretical and ethical motives intertwined in Greek and Hellenistic thought, then it was Christianity which entered upon this inheritance of ancient thought, while *Neo-Platonism* turned back to the old idea that saw in personality only a transitory product of *a life which as a whole is impersonal.* It is the essential feature of the Christian conception of the world that it regards the person and the relations of persons to one another as the essence of reality.[3]

With the religious wealth of the idea of Divine Fatherhood, illuminated and reënforced by the philosophical conception of Perfect Personality, Christianity is singularly equipped to meet the needs of both heart and mind.

When the heart cries out for One sufficient for its deep need, it comes to rest in communion with an All-loving Father; and when the mind seeks a philosophical conception adequate for the intellectual problems arising out of this experience, it is found in the correspondent conception of Supreme Personality.

[3] W. Windelband, *A History of Philosophy,* translation by James H. Tufts, Second Edition, p. 238.

PART II

Adjustments

CHAPTER V

Theology and Divine Fatherhood

The Metaphysical Impulse in Christianity—The Logos furnished to Christianity the constructive Concept for answering the Question: Who is Jesus Christ?—Yet Absorption in the Metaphysical Problem obscured Divine Fatherhood—The Latin Theology substituted Sovereignty for Fatherhood and this Substitution passed over into Protestant Theology—The Rise of a Theology based upon religious Experience restored Fatherhood to its Place in Theology—Yet an Experiential Theology needs Speculation to relate its Truths to expanding Knowledge—Emphasis upon the Divine Immanence, rightly interpreted, has enhanced Fatherhood—The Christocentric Theology, too, has clarified Divine Fatherhood; for instead of deflecting Worship from God the Father, Christ has furnished a Spiritual Lens through whom the Father is seen more truly.

IN PASSING from the New Testament to the period of the great theological controversies, one becomes conscious of a cloud of obscurity gathering about the Fatherhood of God.

At first this seems to be the fault of the metaphysical impulse itself. It is customary on the part of an influential school of modern theology to attribute this element in Christianity to an invasion of Greek thought and to disparage it. This is a hasty and short-sighted judgment. The Greek mind furnished stimulus and form to *absolutely*

Christian philosophical theology, but *the root of a pro-found metaphysic lay in Christianity itself*. For this reason philosophy played an essential part in the development of the Christian Faith. Without it Christianity would have been milk for babes, but not strong meat for men; and both are needed for an adequate religion.

I

The Logos idea supplied the constructive concept for the theological and philosophical interpretation of the new faith. Through it minds like Justin Martyr, and many others far less acute, were won and by means of it they interpreted the new faith to the intellect of the age. Even the orthodox Irenæus and the fervid Tertullian found the Logos doctrine a valuable instrument to interpret and communicate a faith worthy of intellectual as well as moral and spiritual regnancy. That the Logos concept is not only not out of harmony with that of Fatherhood, but helps to clarify and sustain it, is evidenced by its place at the beginning of the Fourth Gospel, through which runs the most intimate and moving representation of God as Father in all literature.

The burning issue which transformed the simple gospel of the Nazarene into a consuming controversial metaphysic was the problem: *Who is Jesus Christ, and how is he related to God and man?* This question lay athwart the path of the Christian religion, inevitable, insatiable, provocative. It is one of the most stimulating, persistent, and productive problems the human intellect ever faced and gave birth to what has proven to be the most earnest, progressive, and fruitful theology which any religion has ever developed. This problem is still engaging the mind of our age. It has led to a searching inquiry into the nature of God and of man and summoned the whole array of philosophical armaments into action. If the Christian Church had not faced this problem, brooded over it, wrestled with it,—and one might almost add, *fought* over it—Christianity might have fallen like a fragile flower of human faith, unable to survive the bleak winds of a hostile intellectualism.

We of to-day may well be grateful that Christianity had within it the possibility of a metaphysic which laid hold of thoughtful minds with an intensity of interest which made the Church the intellectual forum of the post-Augustan age.[1]

II

Yet we are compelled to recognize that the era which gave itself so ardently to this great metaphysical enterprise, in its absorption in doctrinal interests lost touch with the heart of the gospel, drew a veil over the face of the Father, and well-nigh lost sight of the human Jesus in the metaphysical Christ. Those fiery theological serv-

[1] "The intellectual victory of Christianity over all the rival salvations of the time was due to the fact that it alone offered not merely a way of salvation but a philosophy of salvation." George F. Moore, *The Birth and Growth of Religion*, p. 178.

ants of Christ, in trying to define and defend his nature, too often parted with his spirit and fell into barren, loveless, and all but endless controversy. They forgot that "as many as are led by the spirit of God these are the sons of God" and that "if any man have not the spirit of Christ he is none of his." Faint and far upon their strife-filled ears fell the words, so expressive of the spirit of their Master: "By this shall all men know that ye are my disciples, if ye have love one toward another" and "That they all may be one; even as thou, Father, art in me, and I in thee." Foolishly they strained out metaphysical gnats and swallowed moral camels. In the name of Christ they denied him and in striving to maintain the honor of God the Father they dishonored His Fatherhood.

The spirit engendered in the controversial age of Christianity bequeathed to the Christian Church a heritage of intellectualism, dogmatism and espionage which is felt to this day. It has begotten endless heresy trials, intolerance, bigotry, and bitterness. It is the duty of the Christian Church, separating the gold from the dross, to keep the mental discernment, the discrimination, the intellectual values of the age of Christian metaphysics and to renounce the intolerance, and insistence on the primacy of doctrine which have brought so great reproach and hindrance to the Christian faith and well-nigh made the Divine Fatherhood—the initial affirmation of all the great creeds—an empty shibboleth.

III

The Latin theology, though far less metaphysical than the Greek, obscured the truth of Fatherhood even more seriously. Augustine started with quite other premises and purposes from those of the Alexandrians and reached, not a metaphysical Deity, but a Divine Sovereign who is even more remote from the Heavenly Father than the One Essence and three Hypostases. Dominated by the fact of sin, individual and social, and by the need of a powerful institution to control a corrupt and disintegrating civilization, the master mind of his age wrought out a theology peculiarly stamped by the needs and limited vision of the times. Augustine's God—majestic, withdrawn, autocratic, wrapped in His own counsels, condescending to save only a portion of a corrupt race—bears but the most distant resemblance to the Heavenly Father of the Gospels.

Yet there was another side of this remarkable Christian leader and another phase of his theology. Augustine had one God for his theological system and ecclesiastical organization and another for his devotional life. The God of the *Confessions* is as tender, loving, fatherly (as well as infinite and eternal)—One who awakens the deepest adoration of the mystic and satisfies the most urgent mental need of the metaphysician—as the God of the more systematic treatises is remote, governmental, and grandiose. The outcome of this strange blending of contradictory conceptions upon the development of theology was not—as might have been hoped—to dethrone the absolute monarch in favor of the God and Father of our Lord Jesus Christ, but to seat the Sovereign more firmly by attaching to Him attributes impossible to reconcile with His absolute sovereignty by any mind save one like that of Augustine—*e.g.*, his New England successor, Jonathan Edwards.

The inscrutable, absolute Sovereign of Augustinianism passed over into Protestant theology, partially humanized by Luther, but in Calvinism encumbered with the whole legal paraphernalia of decrees, election, the fall, substitutionary atonement, and eternal punishment which hid in somber clouds the true glory of God the Father as revealed in the face of Jesus Christ. How Calvin, with the New Testament in his hands, and the freedom of a new era dawning about him, having broken with the whole corrupt system of ecclesiasticism, could have reproduced the sovereignty theology in a more rigid form than ever —this is something which we of to-day find it hard to understand or to be patient with. Doubtless the political and moral needs of the time were influential in shaping it to this type, yet the first edition of the *Institutes* was published in 1536, before he had started to wrestle with the transformation of Geneva.

The Augustinian-Calvinistic theology of Sovereignty reigned from the fifth century to the rise of modern thought, and has even maintained a sort of decadent prestige to the present time in spite of its disparity with the

New Testament as well as with modern thought.   There have been vigorous insurrections against it—Pelagianism, Socinianism, Arminianism, English Liberalism, Swedenborgianism, Universalism, Unitarianism, the New Theology—but it has persisted, at least formally, in several Protestant communions, ensconced in such iron-clad statements of faith as the Decrees of Dort, the Thirty-nine Articles, and the Westminster Confession.   Yet the Calvinistic system long ago lost its authority outside of a limited ecclesiastical circle and remains only as a survival, like a melting but persistent snowdrift impeding moral and spiritual traffic on the highway of Christian progress.   The Presbyterian Church calls itself Calvinistic but is really mildly Arminian.

It would be short-sighted to underestimate the sovereignty theology, going back, as it does, from Calvin to Augustine, from Augustine to certain Jewish elements in Paul (though not to the real Paul), and from Paul to the historical books of the Old Testament.[2]   There is a regal quality in the idea of a Supreme Father, but an Absolute Sovereign is essentially an anachronism, a survival from the tutelary age of fear and trembling, the glacial epoch in the development of the human spirit.   It obscures the liberating truth which found its great revelation in Him whose whole purpose shines forth in the

[2] "The phrase Almighty God so frequent in the Old Testament never occurs in the New, save once in a quotation from the Old (I Cor. 11:18) and in the Apocrypha.   In the English Prayer Book it is almost invariable."   James Ward, "Faith and Eternal Life," *The Hibbert Journal*, January, 1925, p. 200 (note).

saying: "He that hath seen me, hath seen"—not the Sovereign, but—"the Father."

IV

The reign both of metaphysics and of dogmatics began to break up with the rise of *a theology of experience.* This may be roughly assigned to the appearance of Schleiermacher's *Addresses on Religion* (1799). The new principle slowly but steadily won its way—through the work of Frank, Rothe, Ritschl, Hermann, and others in Germany, Martensen in Denmark, Auguste Sabatier in France, Coleridge, MacLeod Campbell, Maurice, Kingsley, Robertson, in Britain, Henry Ward Beecher, Barnes, Bushnell, Phillips Brooks, Bowne, W. A. Brown, W. N. Clark, in America—until now it is the accepted basis of every progressive theological treatise. The change means much to Christian theology. It reanimates it and restores to it the spirit of reality. It makes of theology a true science—the science of spiritual truth. When religious experience is fully trusted and adequately interpreted no conception answers to it so well as that of One who is as a Father to all men.

The movement in the direction of an experiential theology was held back, however, by another movement which was at its height about the time that Schleiermacher's epoch-making *Addresses* appeared. This was the Rationalism which prevailed in both theology and philosophy during the eighteenth century and continued well into the nineteenth century. As an appeal from authority to reason, Rationalism fulfilled a useful mission. It had neither profundity nor attractiveness, but possessed a certain hard, common-sense sincerity and vigor which wrested the rights of reason from the iron grasp of authority. It sought to justify "natural religion"—or rather a kind of generalized and devitalized theology—at the expense of Christianity by an appeal to reason. It reëmphasized the artificial schism between nature and revelation made by Scholasticism and continued by Protestant Rationalism, whose ill effects Bishop Butler, in his famous *Analogy,* tried to annul by showing that "revelation" presents no greater difficulties than does the system of nature.

Eighteenth-century Rationalism swept both Europe and America, taking the form of the *Aufklärung* in Germany, represented by Wolff, Naturalistic Deism in France, advocated by Voltaire and Rousseau, and Common Sense Deism in England and America, championed by Lord Herbert of Cherbury, Collins, Benjamin Franklin, Ethan Allen, and Tom Paine. God was conceived of by Rationalism as Creative First Cause, Moral Ruler of the Universe—a conception in many ways superior to the Absolute Sovereign of Calvinism and Catholicism, yet having too little of the character of Jesus' "Our Father who art in Heaven."

Rationalism gave way before Romanticism and Pietism. Its cold, academic Deity yielded to the need for a God to love and live with.

V

An experiential theology does not mean, however, the repudiation of reason. The just requirements of reason cannot be set aside. Undifferentiated experience calls for rational interpretation. Fatherhood itself, while emphasizing the experiential relationship, is only an interpretation. Start with the simple relationship which Harnack expressed in the words, "the soul and God, God and the soul," ponder it, probe its meaning and its implications, and you find yourself facing pathways which lead in such diverse directions as Personalism, Pantheism, Absolutism, Deism, and Mysticism.

Problems vast and innumerable arise from even the simplest experience. Proceed from God as experienced, *e.g.*, toward God as Father of the universe, and you find yourself at one time led on by the benign, uniform laws which have made Rationalism so firmly theistic in its conclusions, at another time puzzled and shaken by facts which apparently contradict Divine Fatherhood. These alternating incitements and difficulties cannot be ignored. Starting with experience, theology must seek to understand its implications and to relate it to the facts disclosed by advancing human knowledge. If it succeeds, only in part, it will at least not have avoided the issue. The difference, however, between the theology of the past and that of the present is that the former was at the mercy of every wind that blows, while the latter is firmly and purposefully anchored to experience. Religious experience is now the accepted base of supplies, the source and spring of religious conviction and theological interpretation. If contact with this base is maintained, speculation may travel as freely and as far as it will without becoming starved, impotent, and finally lost.

VI

A second tendency in modern theology has lent support to the doctrine of Fatherhood, while at the same time it receives needed illumination from that doctrine itself— *i.e.,* the emphasis upon *immanence*. It might seem at first thought that Fatherhood implies *transcendence* rather than immanence. But transcendence without immanence is the mark of Sovereignty rather than of Fatherhood. The latter implies both transcendence and immanence—a God who is immanent in His world, yet not as the sap is in the tree, or the blood in the body, or the *élan vital* in the cosmos, but as the poet is immanent in his poem, the architect in his building, the father in the son whom he loves. In other words, the kind of immanence that goes with Fatherhood is an immanence of mind and affection, a spiritual rather than a physical immanence. Personality is immanent in a way of its own, which has its analogue, but not its explanation, in physical immanence. Thus interpreted, Immanence and Fatherhood throw light upon one another. Immanence saves Fatherhood from a remote and external relationship which approximates to Deism and is not true Fatherhood, and Fatherhood saves Immanence from the idea of a mere chemical or vital infusion, which is not true Immanence.

VII

Still another movement in modern theology has given new meaning to Divine Fatherhood. I refer to the Christocentric theology. The Christocentric viewpoint arose, first of all, from the historical study of the life of Jesus. The nineteenth century witnessed a concentration of scholarly and critical research upon the sources of the life of Jesus in its way without a parallel among the achievements of historical and literary science. The result for a time seemed to threaten the historicity of Jesus, but at length issued in a confirmation of the roots of the historical record which leaves it more than ever secure and trustworthy.[3]

Combined with other causes and influences, this historical study has led to a reillumination of the character and teachings of Jesus such that he has become, in the sight of all men, as never before, the ideal of divine-human manhood. And since not only all that he said but all that he was rested upon his reliance upon God as his Father, the latter belief has been brought out in a far stronger and warmer light than ever before. To separate

[3] See A. Schweitzer, *The Quest of the Historical Christ;* Benjamin Bacon, *Introduction to the New Testament;* A. S. Peake, *Commentary on the Bible,* etc.

Jesus from his confidence in God as his Father and the Father of all men, has become more than ever impossible.

Yet this reillumination of the Jesus of history alone is quite insufficient to constitute a Christocentric theology or to furnish a sufficient basis for a fresh faith in Divine Fatherhood.   The Christians of the New Testament gained their inspiration, not simply by regarding Jesus as teacher and exemplar but by finding in his personality spiritual enlightenment and power.   To them he was a unique and incomparable person, a Divine Lord.   Thus there were blended in Christ, both for the early church and for succeeding generations of Christians, the values of a beloved historical individual, possessed of supreme human attraction, and an invisible, eternal, ever-present Spirit—"Christ in you, the hope of glory"—giving us the Jesus of History and the Christ of Faith in One divine-human personality.

The question arises: Does not the Christocentric theology deflect the mind of the Christian from God the Father to God the Son and tend to transform Christianity from the worship of a Divine Father to that of an exalted Christ? The answer lies in the New Testament itself. Here one finds Christ not a substitute for the Father but rather *a spiritual lens,* through whom the face of the Father is seen with a clearness and completeness otherwise impossible.   Principal Fairbairn interpreted the Christocentric theology truly when he described it as Christocentric in method, Theocentric in goal.   Instead

of obscuring the truth of Divine Fatherhood, the Christocentric theology enhances it.

Thus, after moving in various directions away from
God as Father, first toward a metaphysical Substance,
then toward an omnipotent Sovereign, then toward a
semipersonal First Cause, and finally toward an all-inclusive Absolute, theology is now returning—or rather advancing—toward the clear and moving conception
symbolized by Fatherhood and vitalized in Christ.

CHAPTER VI

Philosophy and Divine Fatherhood

The Relation of Philosophy to Theology—Ancient Philosophy approximates Personal Theism—Three Rivals of Theism: Monism, Rationalism, Positivism—The Absolute of Monism, as conceived by Spinoza and later by Hegel, enlarges the Idea of God but deflects from His Fatherhood—Rationalism impoverishes the Fatherhood of God—Positivism offers a Substitute for it—Theism the best general philosophical Interpretation of Divine Fatherhood—Personalism, with its Conception of God as Pure Person, the best proximate Interpretation—Philosophy of great Value but not superior to, or a Substitute for, Religion.

I

IT MIGHT seem at first thought as if Philosophy had little or nothing to do with the conception of God as Father. That might be true if philosophy had nothing to do—as sometimes seems to be the case—with experience. But philosophy, like religion, and its interpreter, theology, *grounds in experience,* although it takes account also—or should—of *that which the mind itself contributes to experience.* Kant recognized both of these factors in knowledge in the well-known and illuminating sentence of the introduction to the *Critique of Pure Reason:* "Al-

83

though all our knowledge begins *with* experience, it by no means follows that it all originates *from* experience."

In some crude fashion every one has a philosophy—ideas about himself, the world, life, God. Far better that this should be, as far as possible, a reasonable philosophy, than an ignorant, erratic, and misleading one. It is foolish to decry metaphysics and fall back upon "common sense." Common sense is good in its place, but *as a philosophy* it is only a euphemism for common ignorance. It is not incumbent upon every man to be a philosopher, but it is incumbent upon him to respect philosophy and its effort to probe and interpret experience. It is quite true that philosophy may err egregiously. For, as said the discerning Shakespeare, "men may construe things, after their fashion, clean from the purpose of the things themselves." Thought has its dangers and deceits, but they are not so great as those that arise from not thinking. We can ill spare philosophy with its great adventure and its wide sweep of wing.

> "What sea-bird o'er the sea
> Is a philosopher the while he goes
> Winging along where the great water throes."

In meeting the problems of knowledge and of reality philosophy finds itself confronted with the question of the knowledge of God as one of its major concerns. Since this is the primary interest of theology, philosophy and theology are, thus far, one enterprise. For this reason they continued in close alliance throughout the ancient and medieval periods and well into the modern.   Closely related as they are, however, they differ in their method of approach to the problem of the existence and nature of God.   Theology approaches the subject more intimately, concerning itself chiefly with religious experience, and interpreting it in terms more symbolic, concrete, and personal; while philosophy concerns itself chiefly with the knowledge of God which arises from the external universe, the structure of the human mind and the nature of knowledge itself, and uses concepts and terms more abstract and universal than those of theology.

II

It is noteworthy that philosophy, from its rise to the present, has maintained, in one of its main currents, a conception of God approximating that of Father.   Both of the greatest minds of ancient philosophy, Plato and Aristotle, approached, though they did not completely reach, Personal Theism.   Plato, in making the Good the chief of the triad of universals—the Good, the True, and the Beautiful—honored the central attribute of Divine Fatherhood and his "Divine Guardian" is a foreshadowing of the Christian conception.   Aristotle's "Unmoved Mover"—conceived as Final Cause—was sufficiently personal to furnish the Schoolmen the basis of their Theism. Stoicism, too, cherished a conception of God which wavers between Cosmic Monism and Theism.   The term "Father" itself appears in Cleanthes' noble hymn to Zeus, closing: "Banish ignorance, O Father, from the souls of men and grant them to obtain wisdom, whereon relying Thou rulest all things with justice."

Yet, while a theistic conception closely allied to Fatherhood has been fostered by philosophy from its beginning, it has not been without powerful rivals. Three great philosophical systems have tended to obscure the conception—Monism, Rationalism, and Positivism. Let us consider briefly the relation of each of these to the idea of Divine Fatherhood.

III

There is something at once fascinating and commanding in the idea of an all-inclusive *Unity*. Whether it arises from the structure and operation of the mind itself, or from the external world, or from both mind and cosmos acting upon each other, in any case the concept of the Whole, or the Absolute, attracts the intellect, calms the emotions, and offers a solution for many perplexities. The philosophy of the Absolute is at once so comprehensive, so rational, and—when so interpreted—so mystical, that to many thoughtful minds it has been both food and drink. For the idea of the Whole readily lends itself to the religious experience.

The religious implications of the idea of Unity furnish the key to the thought-life of India. The Indo-Aryan mind, starting with an elevated form of nature worship, advanced into the profound mysticism of the Upanishads in which the Divine Immanence is so intensely realized that both nature and human personality are at times lost in Brahma, Universal Being. This Absolutism passed over into Mahayana Buddhism, finding expression in such lines as these:

> All things in one and one in all
> Unreal do they pass and fall.
> This path of "oneness" shall ye tread,
> Ye who would free yourselves of dread.[1]

The Transcendental Absolutism of Neoplatonism arrived at a similar result by elevating God above knowledge and attempting to apprehend Him by pure, passive contemplation. Plotinus conceived of God as "the One" —the One being also "the Good," yet so far above what is ordinarily meant by goodness that to term Him Father would be to misconceive Him. Christian Speculative Mysticism, as it appears in Dionysius, Erigena, and others, followed much the same pathway to the Absolute.

That lonely and lofty thinker, Spinoza, discovered in the One Substance, from which flow all forms of existence, a concept at once so majestic in its logical sufficiency and so moving in its appeal to piety that it served him both as philosophy and as religion. His exalted Ethical Monism found deep contentment in a God to be loved with all the mind, Who has all the qualities and attributes to awaken love—save love itself. A Monism which could sustain this solitary, persecuted, "God-intoxicated" thinker cannot be denied ethical and spiritual as well as

[1] K. J. Saunders, *The Essence of Mahayana*, p. 33.

metaphysical values of the highest order for certain exceptional minds.

Hegel, less religious than Spinoza but even more penetrative and inclusive, constructed a Developmental Monism which profoundly influenced the religious, as well as the philosophical, thought of the later nineteenth century. Stimulated by him, Monists of independent insight, like Thomas Hill Green, Edward Caird, Josiah Royce, Bernard Bosanquet, and Henry Jones, have greatly enriched religious as well as philosophic thought.[2] Very closely, at many points, do these synthetic minds approximate to the conception of God as Father. Yet in the end they deflect more or less from it. For God cannot be the All and Father of all, the Absolute and the Object of free devotion, in any but an accommodated sense.

Manifest defects in the interpretation of experience are inseparable from Absolutism. They may be summarized as follows: (1) Absolutism ignores, as Professor James pointed out, certain plain and obstinate facts in the world of empirical experience; (2) it minimizes and sometimes misinterprets moral evil, and (3) it fails to recognize an element in religious experience which is unsatisfied with the idea of the Whole and calls for a more personal and intimate interpretation of spiritual reality. Thus, while Monism has fostered a conception which is essential to Universal Fatherhood, it has tended to substitute the *Idea of Unity* for the *One*.

[2] The entire movement finds its consummation from the point of view of religious inclusiveness and Christian spirit in Sir Henry Jones' truly noble volume, *A Faith That Enquires*.

IV

Sharply contrasted in many respects with Monism, yet placing a like emphasis upon the primacy of thought, is *Rationalism*. Rationalism may be defined as *an extreme reliance upon reason,* or rather, upon *the discursive reason,* to the exclusion of *the intuitive reason.* The discursive reason readily reaches the idea of God as First Cause, or Creative Agency; but its God tends to become the Absentee God of Deism; and God apart from His world has little meaning for humanity. He is not only "without parts or passions," but without spiritual qualities and contacts. Such was the God of Medieval Scholasticism, save as invested with "communicability" by the mysticism of Bonaventura, Aquinas, the Victorines and Dante. Such too was the God of the German *Aufklärung* and of French, English, and American Deism. The incompetence of this view of God to fill out the lineaments of Divine Fatherhood manifestly lies in its failure to recognize immanence as well as transcendence and in the deficiency in its distant Deity of the qualities that inspire communion and affection.

While Monism and Rationalism deflect the mind from Divine Fatherhood by indirection, Positivism offers a distinct substitute for it. Auguste Comte frankly discarded the idea of God as an outgrown and negligible superstition. Built as it is upon the inadequate ideas of the first two of his "three successive stages of thought"

—theological, philosophical, and scientific—Theism, he held, can no longer command the assent of the modern mind. The positive knowledge afforded by science has come, he asserted, to take the place both of theology and of philosophy.

Positivism proved itself unable to bear its own weight. It acknowledged its bankruptcy when Comte turned, dissatisfied, from the barren waste of a purely scientific world to construct his elaborate worship of humanity.[3] Later Positivism has also proven itself a transition philosophy by passing from a world deflowered and robbed of value by a purely scientific outlook to a Naturalism which finds a certain meager food for the religious craving in an all-inclusive *Nature,* within which humanity is swept as into a vast, all-embracing Developmental Experience.[4]

The recent revival of the worship of humanity under the term *Humanism* on the part of some of the representatives of a Christian body one of whose founders was W. E. Channing, recalls a statement made by that great proponent of the dignity of human nature as follows: "I am accustomed to speak of the greatness of human nature, but it is great only through its parentage, great because descended from God." (*Spiritual Freedom,* vol. IV, p. 80.) The moment one turns from *humanity as a*

[3] This was a worship (be it noted) not of humanity in all of its qualities but of the *best* in humanity. Since the highest in humanity may be understood as God immanent in it, such a worship if consistently followed would lead back to immanental Theism.

[4] Naturalism is further discussed in Chapter VII.

whole—calculated in that aspect to inspire compassion rather than worship—to that which is noblest *in* humanity, he is on the way to a God Who is the only adequate explanation of the good in men but Who cannot be the good *in* them unless He is also the Good *above* them.

V

In contrast with these impersonal or semipersonal philosophies, *Theism* offers a conception of God and the world in harmony with the idea of Divine Fatherhood.

Theism has many forms and types.[5] It usually appears in affinity with Dualism, either ethical Dualism, like that of Zoroastrianism, or philosophical Dualism, like that of Descartes.

Ethical Dualism emphasizes a God whose chief characteristics are His moral purity, His abhorrence of evil, and His activity in striving to overcome it—an idea revived, since the war, largely by H. G. Wells' "finite God." Such a God is distinctly personal, and as such has many of the traits of personality. Nevertheless, His very absorption in the moral conflict, His moral militancy, so to speak, is out of keeping with some of the chief characteristics of Fatherhood. Religion will never be wholly content with a God of Battles, even though He battles only with moral weapons and for mankind as a whole. A righteous Father cannot but be intensely engaged, as

---

[5] For a description of various types of Theism see Calderwood's *Philosophy of Religion.*

was the Jahveh of the prophets of Israel, in the struggle for the overthrow of injustice and iniquity; but He is above the battle as well as in it. A clear recognition of moral dualism—the essential antagonism of good and evil—is demanded by the very nature of our experience. But it is not upon this that the *ictus* of Christian philosophy falls, but rather upon the Love which overbroods and underlies the moral conflict.

Philosophical Dualism, more properly termed *Duality*, taking its rise in modern thought with Descartes, is grounded in a fundamental distinction between Matter and Mind, Nature and Spirit. Making this distinction it is able to recognize a Kingdom of God, who is Pure Spirit, and man, who is partial spirit.[6] Monism has failed to dispossess this duality. Nor has either Positivism or Naturalism succeeded in breaking through it; for it rests upon experience. We live in two worlds. Our problem is to bring them into right relationship.

Philosophical Dualism thus provides a setting for Theism; but its emphasis rests upon a contrast which, after all, is but incidental to a larger truth. It fails to give due weight to that central trait of reality—Value. A philosophy of values inevitably places its emphasis upon personality.

---

[6] Realism has appeared as a new form of the duality of subject and object which cannot be permanently ignored. Since Realism, however, throws its whole emphasis upon the object, rather than the subject, it inevitably tends either toward a new form of Materialism or toward Skepticism.

VI

Modern thought has witnessed the development of a philosophy which centers consciously and avowedly in *Personality*—human and divine—as the chief of values and the highest of realities. This makes it the proximate philosophical interpretation of Divine Fatherhood. This philosophy has come to be termed *Personalism*. Its emergence does not mean, of course, that personality has first come to light in modern thought, or that it has not occupied, however implicitly, a leading place in idealistic philosophy.[7]

Plato, Aristotle, and Paul in the ancient world, Descartes, Leibnitz, and Kant in the modern world, have been among the chief architects of the philosophy of personality. Upon the foundations which they and others laid, rests the whole superstructure. Nevertheless, recent philosophy has witnessed a distinctly enlarged and more definite conception of the meaning and worth of personality. This appears in such philosophers as Lotze, Ritschl, Eucken, Troeltsch, in Germany; Renouvier, Maine de Biran, Boutroux, in France; Rashdall, von Hügel, James Ward, Sorley, C. C. J. Webb, James Seth, W. R. Matthews, J. E. Turner, and C. A. Richards, in England; and Ladd, Howison, Bowne, G. H. Palmer,

---

[7] There is much confusion in the use of the term Idealism. While commonly used in the sense of *Idea-ism,* the wider and subtler meaning of *Ideal-ism* hovers about it and makes it the philosophic harbor of all philosophies which lay stress upon the spiritual side of truth.

W. E. Hocking,[8] Mary W. Calkins, J. B. Pratt, E. S. Brightman, H. B. Alexander, J. A. Leighton, G. A. Wilson, R. T. Flewelling, A. C. Knudson, and others, in America. Not all of these would consent to be enrolled as personalists—for there is much to be said against an academic tag—yet all of them have assigned a meaning and value to personality which gives it the leading place in their philosophical systems.[9]

Supreme Personality does not mean that God is *a* Person in the sense of an *individual,* but *the* Person, Pure Person—the Complete Person,[10] "a Cosmic Mind who is working for the conservation and creation of value, and with whom we may be in relations of conscious communion and coöperation." [11] This seems, perhaps, but a dim intellectual *aura* of the familiar conception of a Heavenly Father. Yet it is hardly too much to say that the conception of Infinite Personality as it appears in Lotze's *Microcosmus,* or Bowne's *Personalism,* or Howison's *Limits of Evolution,* or Webb's *Gifford Lectures,* or W. R. Matthews' *Studies in Christian Philosophy* represents approximately the philosophical counterpart of what

[8] Professor Hocking, while in close kinship with Roycean Monism, and making but little use of personalistic terms, seems to me a virtual personalist, as appears in his Immanental Theism and his estimate of values; so, indeed, was Professor Royce himself, although his Monism obscured the full recognition of the Personality of God.

[9] A very clear, concise and well-balanced history and presentation of Personalism has been published by Professor Albert C. Knudson, Dean of Boston University, under the title *The Philosophy of Personalism* (1927).

[10] See my *Personality and the Christian Ideal,* Chapter III, p. 39.

[11] Eugene W. Lyman: "The Rationality of Belief in the Reality of God," *The Journal of Religion,* September, 1922, p. 453.

Jesus meant when he called God: "Our Father who art in Heaven."

VII

Philosophy passes by the imperfect, concrete, familiar, human terms of religion and chooses those which embody reflection, universality, differentiation. Does not this show its superiority to religion? Would it not be better —avoiding much misunderstanding and the danger of making the thought of God commonplace—if, instead of calling God *Father,* we should substitute the name *Infinite Personality* or *Supreme Person?* Our answer, as earlier in the discussion, is: No. Such designations are of service but they are too abstract, too academic, too remote from human interests and everyday values, to serve more than a restricted usage.

Philosophy is philosophy. It has its own appropriate categories, terms, modes of thought, and expression. It has its own office in the hierarchy of human interests. Yet it has its limitations also. If not "too bright nor good for human nature's daily food," it is too insubstantial, detached, and abstract. This does not involve any disparagement of philosophy in its proper place. Its values for human use are inestimable. It supplies not only nectar and ambrosia for Olympians, but wholesome food and drink for human nature's occasional, if not its daily diet; yet it does not furnish a dietary sufficient to maintain the average man in health and harmony of mind and soul. There are not enough vitamines in it for that. This is the function of religion, not of philosophy.

Nevertheless, philosophy is called upon to examine and amplify what religion and theology have to say of God. In this capacity it clarifies the conception of Fatherhood, lending to it greater significance and wider marginal meanings. To conceive of God as Supreme Person serves to indicate how complete is His nature and how multiform and universal are His relationships.[13]

It means much to have a vital and clear-visioned school of philosophy in harmony with Christianity in finding in Supreme Personality (the philosophical equivalent of Fatherhood) the amplest, most enduring, most rational solution of the problem of Ultimate Reality. Yet it would be a mistake to infer that only the personalist in philosophy can consistently hold the truth of Divine Fatherhood in religion. On the contrary Monism, Pragmatism, Realism, and other philosophies may each contribute to the conception of Divine Fatherhood, if its particular conception of truth is not raised to such prominence that it not only obscures but absorbs every other. All genuine philosophies work together for good to them that love God, each revealing something of the height of His transcendence, or the intimacy of His immanence, or the breadth of His relationships, or the depth of His nature.

[13] For an illuminating discussion of the present relations of philosophy to religion see Professor Muirhead's Introduction to the second volume of his *Contemporary British Philosophy*.

CHAPTER VII

Natural Science and Divine Fatherhood

The Effect of Nature upon Religious Faith sometimes stimulating, at other times adverse—Science requires that Nature be dissociated from Religion and examined by Itself; yet Science and Religion are inherently friendly and remained so until Ecclesiasticism forced them apart; then Science became isolated and self-sufficient—The Startling Revelation of the Great War that Science may serve destructive and degrading Ends—Inferences from Science which have successively arisen to discredit Religion; Materialism and Agnosticism decadent; Naturalism now in the Ascendant—Nature constantly discloses new Aspects and Indications which point beyond herself toward Supernature.

I

NATURE—intending by this word of many meanings the external world, including its relation to sensation—has been both teacher and temptress of man, his inspiration and his undoing, according to his attitude toward her.

In her more gracious and benign aspects, Nature has sometimes fostered, sometimes absorbed, religion. When she has nourished and delighted Manchild, he has either taken her bounty and beauty as the expressions of a Divine Goodness which fills him with gratitude and devotion; or else he has allowed these satisfactions to satiate and sodden him. When she has withheld her gifts in drought, or blight, or has struck him down with plague or tempest, flood or earthquake, he has either interpreted these disasters as expressions of Divine displeasure and been moved by them to penitence and closer fellowship with his deity, or he has been hardened by them into bitterness, resentment, and skepticism.

Only the insight of a few noble and discerning souls has been able so far to detach external ills and losses from the resources of the inner life as to find compensation for the loss of outward satisfactions in the solace of a pure and victorious faith, as *e.g.* Habakkuk, when he sings:

> For though the fig-tree shall not flourish,
> Neither shall fruit be in the vines;
> The labor of the olive shall fail,
> And the fields shall yield no food;
> The flock shall be cut off from the fold,
> And there shall be no herd in the stalls;
> Yet I will rejoice in Jehovah,
> I will joy in the God of my salvation.

II

It seems to be essential to the advancement of science to distinguish somewhat sharply between Nature and Spirit, to dissociate God from Nature, at least so far as to see that, whatever the relationship between them, they must first be understood by themselves, each in its own sphere.

Natural science from its beginning has been largely conditioned upon making this distinction. Only as this has been done has progress in the knowledge and use of Nature become possible. It was not until inquiring minds began to segregate natural phenomena and let them tell their own story freely and independently that fruitful results began to appear. That this was so long delayed was the fault, not of religion, but of a theological mis-reading of religion which identified it with certain traditions and doctrines which appeared to ban any independent examination of natural phenomena.[1] The earlier adventures in science showed no disposition to be hostile to religion, but rather the reverse. Nor did modern science begin with any opposition toward religion, but rather in sincere recognition of its priority. This may be observed in Roger Bacon's correspondence with Pope Clement IX, in the reverent attitude toward the Church of Copernicus and Galileo, and later in the unfaltering theism of Francis Bacon's works, the earnest piety of Newton's *Principia,* and in the deeply religious spirit of such scientists as Faraday, Boyles, Kepler, Lyell, Dana, Agassiz, and many others.[2]

[1] Cf. Andrew D. White: *The Warfare of Science with Theology.*

[2] In Sir Francis Bacon's *New Atlantis* the head, or "father," of *Solomon's House,* after describing the extraordinary appliances for scientific discovery in every field contained therein, adds: "We have certain hymns and services which we say daily, of laud and thanks to God for his marvellous works. And forms of prayers, imploring his aid and blessing for the illumination of our labours; and turning them into good and holy uses."

Ecclesiasticism and dogmatic theology—in the name, but not in the spirit, of Christianity—affronted and chilled this friendly attitude, which might otherwise have continued and developed into an unbroken alliance of religion and science. Finding the conclusions of scientific study out of harmony with Scripture, as interpreted in theological systems, the official representatives of the Church chose to block the progress of science and to condemn her own scientists. Thus began a misunderstanding, ripening into a long and often bitter conflict. This has been wrongly termed a conflict between science and religion, whereas it was really a conflict between science and theology, or rather between science and what might well be termed *theologism*. The rupture grew into a wide and dismal chasm into which not a little honest faith has fallen and been lost.

It is not difficult to see how religion lost ground through this misunderstanding. With the rapid advance of science in the nineteenth century came a period when the concentration of attention upon scientific achievements made Nature seem very real and responsive and the spiritual world increasingly unreal and remote. With the advent of Evolution it began to seem as if the natural order were a self-sufficient system. Nature was witnessed at work apparently creating her own forms and variations, producing species out of genera, genera out of simpler forms, and all out of a few, perhaps a single, life substance. Thus at length the entire process appeared as a self-producing and self-perpetuating whole, with no room left for God and His activity.

As the fruits of applied science multiplied, satisfying all the physical needs of humanity, conquering disease, providing new objects of interest and entertainment, making life rich in comfort, ease, and pleasure, the question arose: What need more for religion? It seemed to many—not all superficially minded—that the time had come for religion to retire from the stage—an outworn and discredited survival of an unscientific age.

III

The Great War came and tested these assumptions, as by fire. The very instruments and achievements of science became implements of destruction, fiendish devices for the torture and death of the peoples who had invented them. The lesson was branded deep upon both body and soul. Slowly, sternly, with terrible realism, it became evident that man cannot live by science alone, that to build up a material civilization without spiritual culture adequate to purify motive and direct human activity means, in the end, to prepare the ground for greed, enmity, war, destruction.

Nor was it simply the domination of the destructive and war-provoking by-products of science that became appalling, but the accompanying paralysis of human ideals and motives. The truth began to dawn upon discerning minds before the war, and has been becoming

clearer ever since, that life, nurtured upon physical resources alone, becomes loathsomely "weary, stale, flat,
and unprofitable." The "ghastly, smooth life, dead at
heart," has stared our generation in the face, and in its
pallid emptiness, it has been seen, as men have never seen
it before, that "the mind of the flesh is death." The
bankruptcy of life dominated solely by material ends, in
which men struggle for the largest share of the spoils of
applied science,—crushing labor in industrial slavery,
piling up great armaments for the defense of acquired
gain, indifferent to the higher values of life, has become
so poignantly, overwhelmingly, clear to our generation
that we are being driven to turn to something that science
cannot furnish, in order to save, not only our souls, but
the very civilization that we have inherited and which
we fondly imagined was secure for all time.

It would, of course, be wholly incorrect and unjust to
lay the blame for this state of moral and spiritual deca-
dence upon science as such. It is not pure science, but
science exaggerated, exploited, worshiped, that is responsible. The way out is clear. From all directions—
from statesmen, philosophers, men of affairs, laboring
men, professional men, business men, and scientists
themselves—has come a united expression of the conviction that it is only religion, or more specifically Christianity, that can save our civilization. Nothing less can
give to our generation a fresh realization of supreme
values, a new sense of the soundness of personal and

social relations, and a renewed confidence in the Power not ourselves that makes for righteousness.

IV

As if to further the trend toward religion, the inferences from science which have seemed to discredit religion are rapidly disappearing. This appears as one glances backward at the failure of the successive philosophical substitutes for religion which have attached themselves to science as if they were its rightful kindred and exponents.

The first of these was *Materialism.* Materialism is almost as old as the earliest attempts to understand Nature. It found voice in Democritus, with his theory of uncreated monads, later in the *De Natura Rerum* of Lucretius, later still in Hobbes, La Mettrie, and Condillac. It took a fresh lease of life from nineteenth-century science as interpreted by Ernst Haeckel in his *Riddle of the Universe.* For a time it seemed to be in the ascendant; but as scientific investigation opened up wider aspects of Nature, especially as science began to probe deeper into the minute and invisible, Materialism became too crude and smug a theory to account for the activities and processes of Nature. Science is now engaged in reviewing and revising long accepted but hitherto unexamined concepts. "At its moment of supreme success its limitations disclose themselves and call for a renewed exercise of the creative imagination." [3] The theory of

---

[3] A. N. Whitehead, *Science and the Modern World*, p. 292.

Relativity has brought unexpected implications, almost consternation, to unreflective science. As Lord Haldane has pointed out, "the theory of relativity has brought us to see that the part which the mind plays in the fashioning of knowledge of what we call facts is larger than we had supposed."

Yet long before Einstein appeared, Materialism, except in its practical form, had spent its force. For a time *Agnosticism* took its place. Agnosticism is less narrow and dogmatic than Materialism. Sponsored by such minds as Spencer and Huxley, it overflowed the confines of mere Materialism. Such men were too sensitive and wide-visioned to deny the existence of Something beyond matter. They relegated this Something, however, to the realm of the Unknowable; and the Unknowable proved too intangible to play the part. Hence the advance to *Naturalism.*

As the ever widening range of physical activity and potentiality has absorbed, or seemed to absorb, within itself more and more of the domain not only of life but of mind, Nature has come, for many minds, to fill the whole horizon. Many of those who sit daily at her gates have come to believe that Nature is sufficient to account for everything—mindless yet producing mind, unconscious yet producing consciousness, nonsocial yet producing society, nonreligious yet producing religion. Beyond her lies—*nothing.* Naturalism is, of course, closely akin to Materialism, but its horizons are wider. It is more absorbed in the dynamic, organic, evolving nature of reality.

Its mechanism is the mechanism of an organism, not of a machine.

Naturalism rests to a large extent upon inferences and deductions from science, but in no sense upon science itself. Although seeming to have all the prestige of science supporting it, it is an extrascientific theory. Persuasive, impressive, appealing to the imagination more than either Materialism or Agnosticism, untroubled by any "blank misgivings of a creature moving about in worlds not realized," Naturalism daily extends its sway over a generation released from all bondage to established belief yet desiring something to take the place of God.

How widespread and influential Naturalism, in various forms, has become can hardly be realized until one observes what a strong hold it has won upon contemporary philosophy and psychology. One may instance the Æsthetic Naturalism of Santayana, the Experiential Naturalism of Dewey (appearing as a fresh development of his philosophy in *Experience and Nature*),[4] the "Logi-

---

[4] "Man is within Nature, a part of its interactions," writes Dewey. Yes, within Nature physically, but beyond and above her mentally and spiritually. Dewey's Naturalism has in it much of his earlier Idealism, as Santayana has pointed out in a brilliant review of *Experience and Nature* (*The Journal of Philosophy*, XXII, No. 25). In his exalting of the immediate, Santayana charges Dewey with a kind of metaphysical mysticism. "The immediate is, indeed, recognized and prized only by mystics, and Dewey himself is assured of possessing it only by virtue of his social and ethical mysticism, by which the whole complex theater of contemporary action seems to him to be given immediately" (p. 684). Dewey has replied to Santayana, closing thus: "When he [Santayana] lets himself go in any body of subject-matter, free from the influence of traditional and professorial labels, I not only learn much from him, but I flatter myself that I am for the most part in agreement with him. But when he deals with a system of thought and finds

cal Atomism" of Bernard Russell,[5] the Developmental
Agnostic Realism of Samuel Alexander, and the new Psychological Naturalism.

The psychological phase of Naturalism exhibits it in
its most extreme and self-refuting consequences. The
Selfless Psychology of to-day appears to exult in reducing
human beings to mere *automata*. It would revise Shakespeare's apostrophe of man to read somewhat as follows:
What a piece of work is man! how weak in reason! how
strong in instincts! in form and moving how reflex and
mechanical! in action how like an ape! in behavior how
like an ameba! the dupe of all the world! the animal of
animals! [6]

V

These Nature philosophies—Materialism, Agnosticism,
Naturalism—all claiming science as their basis and support, are finding science herself working their undoing.

it necessary to differentiate his own system from it, his naturalism
reduces itself to a vague gesture of adoring faith in some all-compre-
hensive unknowable in contrast with which all human life—barring this
one gesture—is specious and illusory. . . . The case seems to resemble
that of the Irishman who said the two men looked very much alike,
especially one of them. Barring that feature of Mr. Santayana's thought
to which exception has been taken, I am happy to be that one."
Journal of Philosophy, XXIV, 3, p. 64.

[5] Russell thus entitles his philosophy in J. H. Muirhead's *Contemporary
British Philosophy*, vol. I.

[6] The advocates of a Selfless Psychology, while they are at one in
disposing of the self as a relic of Introspective Psychology, are at odds
among themselves to account for the phenomena formerly attributed to
selfhood. *Cf.* J. W. Buckham, *Personality and Psychology.*

They are too meager and limited to interpret so rich a content of reality as Nature presents. Science has been unfolding aspects of Nature which, upon the testimony of scientists themselves, point the way toward wider presciences and postulates than it can explain. The range of mechanism has been greatly extended, but it is quite possible, as Lotze suggested, that mechanism may be the very best instrument of Purpose. "We thank whatever gods may be for a mechanism on which we can absolutely depend. . . . So much we may cheerfully concede to the mechanistic view. We will give it the earth and stars as well. But is it all? Is there no room left for personalism in the universe? Is there no place and no way in which there is adjustment to personal needs or to personal worth?" [7]

Matter, with its elements and substances, and even its indivisible atoms, has resolved into those invisible, unresting will-o'-the-wisps, electrons. A well-known physicist of the University of California wrote a few years ago, as follows:

Some of the most remarkable triumphs of the scientific imagination belong to our own time. Thirty years ago physical science seemed to have reached its limit. Many physicists believed that no further advance was possible except more exact descriptions of known phenomena. There were speculations, of course, but they seemed to be beyond the range of experimental verification. Mach, Pearson, Ostwald, and others, actuated by a praiseworthy but somewhat exaggerated

[7] Willard Brown Thorp, *Mechanism or Personalism.*

spirit of caution, challenged all conclusions which could not be verified by the direct evidence of the senses. Even the atomic theory, fruitful as it had been in physics and chemistry, was abandoned by Ostwald because he could not see atoms. Then by a happy chance X-rays were discovered, and this led to a closer investigation of the cathode rays which excite them. Imagination once more plucked up courage and helped J. J. Thomson to find the electron and to prove it a negatively charged body much smaller than the hydrogen atom. Then came the discovery of radioactivity, which at first completely baffled the physicists. The daring imagination of Ernest Rutherford suggested an explanation which seemed like sacrilege to some of the older physicists, to whom the idea of the indivisibility of the atom had the sanctity of a religious creed. He explained radioactivity as the effect of the explosive disintegration of atoms, and conclusively verified this hypothesis. We can now easily show effects produced by single atoms in such convicing ways that even Ostwald has renewed his allegiance to the atomic theory. We can weigh atoms, measure the charges they carry, and count the number in a given quantity of matter as accurately as the grocer can weigh a pound of sugar or count the number of potatoes in a bushel. We have a fairly satisfactory, but still admittedly incomplete, picture of the atom as a small positively charged nucleus with electrons revolving around it. With the aid of alpha particles shot from radioactive substances with tremendous velocities, Rutherford has been able to disintegrate atoms and produce on a small scale the transmutation of elements vainly attempted by the alchemists. . . . These discoveries have opened a new world to the imagination of those who study science, a world entirely inaccessible to our sense perceptions.[8]

[8] Professor E. P. Lewis, Scientific Imagination, *The University of California Chronicle,* July, 1925, p. 257.

Neither Materialism nor Agnosticism can live in such a universe as this. Materialism is too restrictive; Agnosticism is too negative and hesitant. Agnosticism, in its Spencerian form, long ago betrayed its inconsistency, under the searching criticism of James Ward and others, before the manifest truth that to claim to know nothing of an acknowledged and puissant Reality called the Unknowable is to deny and affirm in the same breath.[9] Since that time its inadequacy has become increasingly evident.

Even Naturalism, in the light of recent science, is coming to seem dogmatic and provincial. There are more things in heaven and earth than are dreamt of in its philosophy. The closing of doors to what may lie either within or beyond nature is a palpable dogmatism. The philosophy of "Look no farther" is self-defeating. "Halt here!" is a sign which the human mind will not long heed.

Viewed in the light of what she conceals, as well as what she reveals, Nature keeps the mind incessantly searching and voyaging. By means of her nonfinalities, her limitations, her intimations, she protests against deification and points beyond herself for the secret of her potencies and the solution of her enigmas. Nature, by her very nature, is not the Ultimate. To stop with her is to allow the mental to yield to the nonmental; it is to take a wayside inn for the end of the road. Beyond lie Mind, Soul, Spirit. Science herself points to Super-

[9] Cf. Ward's *Naturalism and Agnosticism.*

science; Nature predicates Supernature. "On ne comprend la terre que lorsqu' on a connu le ciel. Sans le monde religieux le monde sensible offre une enigme desolante." [10]

[10] "One does not understand the earth until he knows heaven. Without the world of religion the world of sense presents a desolating enigma." Joubert, *Pensées,* I, vii.

CHAPTER VIII

Mysticism and Divine Fatherhood

Mysticism a Deliverance from Intellectualism and the Bondage of Formulas and Conventions—The literary Fruitage of Mysticism—The Freedom with which the Mystic employs his own Names for the Supreme Reality—Most of these Terms intrinsically consistent with Fatherhood—The Failure of Esoteric Religion to appreciate the Concept Father for God—The Value of the Concept of Divine Fatherhood in restraining Mysticism from Irrationality, emotional Excess, and Sentimentality.

THE human mind is in perpetual danger of becoming the slave of its concepts, processes, and terminologies. We are prone to fancy that after conceiving, describing, and naming our experiences we have exhausted them. This danger is a constant attendant of philosophy, science, and theology. Philosophy is an essential and noble pursuit, but it has three serious defects: It lacks the sense of mystery, the sense of humor, and (too often) the sense of value. The same is true of science. These are serious deficiencies. For we live not by knowledge alone but also by emotion, imagination, and affection.

The danger of being swamped by formulas and conventions is greatest and most serious in the interpretation of

religion.   For here the baneful effect of barren intellectualism is most felt.

I

From this imprisoning of experience in formulas, this
drying up of the sources of knowledge, this circumscrib-
ing of the bounds of reality, Mysticism offers unfailing
and welcome deliverance.   "It is necessary now and
then," writes Rudolf Otto, "to melt down, as it were, the
human lineaments of God in the more elemental entirety
of the original experience." [1]   Mysticism does this and is
thus forever freeing the human spirit from self-bondage,
breaking through confining walls, opening new doors,
pouring fresh air into enclosed areas and anointing the
imagination for further flights.   It finds expression in
poetry, art, worship.   "Don't let the poets falter," warned
Francis Childs, "I don't value the philosophers very
much . . . their talk frightens me like ghost stories.
When I go back to the poets I realize I have been
fooled." [2]   No, not fooled but *stinted*.

The practicalist and the literalist—not to say the scientist and the philosopher—are puzzled and put out by
Mysticism.   Poetry, art, religion seem to them to lie
upon the fringes of life.   It is a serious mistake.   Life
is a dreary thing without imagination, emotion, reverence.

[1] *The Idea of the Holy;* English translation by J. W. Harvey, p. 203.
[2] *Atlantic Monthly,* July, 1923, p. 84.

The mystic is, in fact, indispensable. Especially do we
need him to save us from conventional and lifeless ideas
of God. And this he is ever ready to do. Intrepidly, un-
weariedly, he challenges every idea of God, old and new,
accepted or tentative, and every name for Him, metaphysical or moral, rational or affectional, including that
of "Father." To the whole company of philosophers and
theologians, he cries: Why do you attempt to confine
God within the narrow bounds of "Creator," "First
Cause," "Unmoved Mover," "Designer," "Moral Gover-
nor," "the Almighty," "the Eternal," "the Absolute," "the
Trinity," "Supreme Personality," or even "the Father"?
He cannot be thus cabin'd, cribb'd and confin'd. He over-
flows all these designations, and obliterates them.

Through all fixed ideas and congealed terms Mysticism
has made its way, like the spring sunshine that releases
the ice-bound streams of the intellectual Northland. In
place of conventions the mystic has dared to substitute
ideas and terms so large, so undetermined, so expansive,
that they seem to have no definite meaning at all, to be
scornful of confinement to an idea. His imaginings loom
like mountains into the clouds or fade like iridescent
mists into the dazzling purity of blinding light. Mysticism seizes ideas which suggest but do not define, and
adopts names that challenge or even affront thought—
the Abyss, the Unknown, the Fünkelein, the Beyond that
is within, Nothing. Hugo of St.-Victor taught that God
can be better conceived by negative than by positive

expressions.   Suso called God "a nameless Nothingness, a Not of all the things which man can think or say." [3]

The mystic has climbed the Delectable Mountains.   He has escaped from the weary, decrepit, sin-stained world into a realm of eternal youth, where all is new.   "For we have sinned and grown old," exclaims the wise and childlike Chesterton, "and our Father is younger than we."

Mysticism is, in fact, happily inconsistent, often incoherent, in its attitudes and deliverances.   It exults in this inconsistency.   It sets out with the declaration that the realities experienced are too great, too wondrous, too ineffable to be described.   And then it seizes all sorts of extravagant and daring concepts, symbols, metaphors, hyperboles, with which to recall and communicate the experience, and ends by insisting once more that it is too full of meaning to be related or expressed, that it is sacrilege to think to describe it, yet that it is too tremendous to be silent about.

This does not mean that because mystical experience is emotionally and imaginatively vivid it is intellectually weak.   It is anything but that; although its intellectual action is often too rapid and intense to be successfully recorded in exact terms.   The mystic's thoughts and feel-

---

[3] Höffding, *Philosophy of Religion,* p. 81.

Dionysius speaks of the One Perfect as "superessentialiter superessentialis superdivinitas."   Erigena writes, "Negation is in fact the superior quality, affirmation the inferior."   Cf. "The Speculative Mysticism of Dionysius, Erigena and Jacob Boehme," *The Review of the Churches,* April, 1926.

ings are volatile. They "break through language and escape"; yet they often leave a precious literary deposit.

II

For, with all its freedom from formality and premeditated activity, Mysticism has produced many masterpieces of literary art. It is sufficient to recall Plato's *Phœdrus* and *Symposium,* gems "of purest ray serene"; the *Bhagavad Gita* and the *Fourth Gospel,* bright particular stars in the firmament of literature; the *Enneads* of Plotinus, with their large and commanding rationality stirring the mind as well as the soul; Augustine's *Confessions,* food for thought as well as devotion; Dante's *Divina Commedia,* as noble in structure as it is fervid in feeling; George Herbert's love lyrics of *The Temple,* which not only please the fancy and kindle the heart but gratify the intellect; Bunyan's *Pilgrim's Progress,* possessing an unaccountable literary grace, as if written by one long tutored in schools of whose very existence he was hardly aware; Francis Thompson's *The Hound of Heaven,* consummate art as well as devout and daring mysticism. The best mystical literature, moreover, with all its warmth and fervor, never offends the canons of good taste. It keeps the mental powers alert and active, yet it never aims at this but secures it by an admirable indirection. The literature of Mysticism makes its appeal, not to the fastidious mind but to the normal mind. One may instance such classic texts of Mysticism as the sermons of

Eckhart and Tauler, which, by their homely sincerity and
profundity, won the common man, stirring sluggish currents of reflection of whose existence within him he was
hardly conscious.

Here lies the secret of the fadeless bloom of the Bible.
Nothing could be more significant than the strength and
permanence of its appeal, not only to the cultured but to
the unlettered and unschooled, who dumbly feel its
strength and beauty as well as its truth.   Luther's translation of the Scriptures into German and Tyndale's into
English aroused the common people to the realities of a
spiritual kingdom hid from the wise and prudent but
revealed to babes.   No ignorance is more profound or
more pitiful than that which scorns the power to understand the deepest truth that lies hidden in the mind of
the common folk.   Jesus affords the incomparable example of confidence in the power of the unsophisticated man
to understand the things of the Spirit.

III

The true mystic is freely eclectic.   He takes, without
fear or favor, whatever symbol or analogy of spiritual
truth serves him, and lays hold of whatever word moves
him, in order to express the indefinable Reality who is
"closer than breathing and nearer than hands or feet."
Spirit, Christ, the Father, the Beloved, Way, Light,
Truth, Love, Shepherd, King, Savior, Friend—all names
for the Divine serve; none suffices.

This freedom in the use of concepts for spiritual realities appears in the New Testament. "The indwelling
divine is spoken of by John, now as God, again as Christ,
and again as the Spirit."[4] Paul is still freer in his inter-
change of terms. Christ, Jesus, the Lord, the Spirit—
how fully and interchangeably he uses these names!

Seems unfair to me

The Friends have adopted as their customary designation for the Supreme Being, *Spirit,* and have found in
it an inspiring name for God; but they mean by it no
other than Him whom Jesus called Father. Many an
individual Christian has his own favorite designation for
the Great Companion. One will say "Father," another
"Spirit," another "Lord," another "Christ." An honored
friend of mine, of mature Christian experience, almost
invariably called the Unseen Friend, to whom his soul
was bound, not "Father" but "Christ." It was, of course,
the Spirit Christ, the Christ of Experience rather than
the Jesus of History (although closely allied with him),
who held this place in his mind and heart. A more consistent use of names and terms may be desirable, but
freedom is better than rigidity. Nor can it be argued
that one is in the right and another in the wrong in his
theology because of the terms employed.

Not a Trinitarian

this chap. is the book

why not?

IV

Our working religious concepts and ideas—when we
are using them for service and not for display—are, in

[4] McGiffert, *Op. cit.,* p. 37.

fact, strikingly and, on the whole, happily, free and inconsistent. Men of the most orderly and inherently self-consistent thinking cherish ideas of God singularly out of keeping with one another. Yet there are two kinds of inconsistency. One is on the surface and allows room for the interplay of varied and contrasted aspects of truth, each of which, like the facets of a diamond, has its own hue, while all flash together in one sparkling radiance. The other inconsistency is that of inner clash and contradiction, reflecting an inherent irreconcilability.

To think of God as both Father and Son is an extrinsic inconsistency which, when it is understood, only adds to our better understanding of Him; but to think of Him both as Father and Absolute Sovereign, both as Loving and Hating, both as Personal and Impersonal, both as One and Many, both as All and Above All, is to foster intrinsic inconsistencies which offend intellectual and moral integrity and reduce thought to chaos.

For Mysticism as for metaphysics the term Father, taken alone, is insufficient. In order to keep the idea of God expansive and spiritual enough for the mystical mind, the name Father needs to be supplemented with other ideas and names which amplify yet do not contradict it. Its boughs are wide and lofty enough to harbor the flock of meanings that fly instinctively to it.

One of the best of the mystical conceptions of God is that of Spirit. Surely there is nothing incongruous between "Father" and "Spirit." On the contrary, there is the greatest harmony between them, provided *Spirit* be

used in a sufficiently spiritual sense, and *Father* in a sufficiently fatherly sense.   Indeed, the author of the Fourth
Gospel makes Jesus use the terms Spirit and Father as
practically synonymous, as in the familiar words to the
woman at the well: "God is a Spirit: and they that worship him must worship him in spirit and in truth," immediately following the saying: "The hour cometh, and now
is, when the true worshippers shall worship the Father
in spirit and in truth."   "Spirit," "Father"—are they not
both inadequate attempts to express that which no name
can express?   Yet both awaken a response which witnesses to the Reality for which they stand.   "Friend,"
too, is one of the legitimate terms in which the mystic
dares address God.   It is as thrilling as it is daring and
brings God nearer without affront.   Yet who is a truer
Friend than a Father?

Another name for God which the mystic cherishes is
Love.   Indeed, this is a Biblical term, found in the memo-
rable word, "God is Love." [5]   Why not, then, choose Love
as the best term for God, rather than Father?   Because
Father means all that Love means and conveys besides, in
a concrete personal form, that which the abstract term
Love—gracious and meaningful as it is—cannot express.
"Father" means that God is Lover as well as Love.

The mystics are right in seizing every name and analogy which makes God more real, without degrading Him.
Yet, in the end, the God of the Christian mystics, by
whatever swift, original, intimate pathway He is reached

[5] I John 4:8.

and however variously He is conceived and named, is seen to be in harmony with, and in no case superior to, "Our Father."

V

A line is sometimes drawn between exoteric and esoteric religion, between the nonmystic and the mystic, the partially enlightened and the fully enlightened. Those who draw this line conceive that to think of God as Heavenly Father is true and best for those who have not entered into the full knowledge of the Ineffable One; but for those who have tasted of the Hidden Manna, who have passed within the Veil, the Nameless One must remain Nameless, or be given a more mysterious title than Father.

There are two serious objections to this esoteric conception of religion. The first is that it discredits the mysticism of Jesus, who seems to have found in the concept Father room for the full range of the mystical experience. If we may trust his usage, the relation of Father and Son expresses the most perfect spiritual intimacy and union possible. "Believest thou not that I am in the Father and the Father in me?" "I and the Father are One." Such sayings express all that that favorite metaphor of mystical literature, Bridegroom and Bride, conveys and do so in a symbolism incapable of misinterpretation. The second objection to esoteric mysticism is that it discredits the rational and practical elements in religion, both of which have as essential a place as feeling. It is of the nature of true religion to be as universal as sunlight, as free as air, as vital as the growing grass and the leafing tree, as high as heaven and as deep as the sea, yet as simple as the relation of child and Father.

VI

In breaking through the stereotyped terms and conventional forms of religion and lending it freedom and vitality, the service of Mysticism is inestimable. Without it religion would become, what in fact it often has become, barren, lifeless, conventional. Yet in performing this service it should not be forgotten that Mysticism itself is in jeopardy—that of losing hold of the rational and moral elements which are, in their way, as essential to true religion as the mystical element. Once let go of these and Mysticism fades into a passive quietism or evaporates into a meaningless ecstasy. When this occurs prophecy is drowned in "speaking with tongues," intellect is submerged in emotion, moral balance is lost in excitement, thought is swallowed up in contemplation. Such mysticism is apt to lose its anchorage. It parts company with rational thinking. Its sense of ethical and social obligations grows weak. It forgets to serve. It loses the Bodhisattva in the Arahat. It yields the disciple to the recluse. It loses the human touch. The greatest mystics have never made this mistake—neither Jesus nor Gautama, Paul nor Augustine, Benedict nor St.

a strange friendship companionship?

Francis, Bernard nor Zinzendorf, John Fox nor William Cary, Catherine of Genoa nor Eckhart, Tauler nor Jacob Boehme, the Cambridge Platonists nor Wesley, Frederick Robertson nor David Livingstone, John G. Whittier nor Phillips Brooks, nor any other of the great constructive and serviceable mystics.

The conception of God as Father—thus is our conclusion—needs the freedom and enrichment of Mysticism, with its unfettered ideas, warm affections, and glowing imagination, to keep it from conventionality and commonplaceness and to lend it emotional vividness and imaginative scope; and Mysticism needs the restraint, the normality, the rationality, the human tenderness and strength of the conception of God as Father to keep it from irrationality, emotional excess, and vapid sentimentality.

There is a saying of an ancient philosopher—was it Heraclitus?—whose sagacity and insight lend it peculiar pertinence: *"There is One who is unwilling, yet willing, to be called Zeus."* There is One who is unwilling, to be called "Our Father"—*unwilling* if this familiar name is permitted to confine Him to too narrow bounds, but *willing* if thereby His wisdom and justice, and the strength and tenderness of His love may be more fully realized.

PART III

Obstacles

CHAPTER IX

The Dark Side of Nature

Is the Dark Side of Nature or the Bright Side the more significant?—It will help to answer this Question to note certain Conclusions concerning Nature which Man has slowly reached: (1) Natural Events are not the direct Acts of God—(2) Evolution throws Light on the Imperfections in Nature—(3) The Recognition of Germinal Freedom, in different Degrees, throughout Animate Nature helps to account for the Variety of Devices for maintaining Life among living Creatures—Nature in Process indicates a progressive Creative Intelligence, as seen, *e.g.,* in animal Instinct—Viewed as culminating in Human Personality, the Dark Side of Nature loses much of its Somberness.

THE majesty and beauty of the world have been pressing in upon the souls of men, or furnishing "room for the imprisoned splendor to escape"—or both—for countless generations. Ever brighter, more beautiful, glows the face of Nature, charming the child, inspiring the poet, awakening the artist, winning all who have the open vision. "I am related to all that I see," cried Fichte, "and all that I behold respires with inner meaning."

The ministry of Nature becomes not only constantly fuller of æsthetic delight but more contributive to the inner life of man. The subtler and more spiritual side of Nature is finding its way more and more into human ex-

perience. The faintest star that shines, the dullest dawn
that breaks, the lowliest bird that sings, as well as the
meanest flower that blows, can "awaken thoughts that do
often lie too deep for tears"; too deep for tears because
they lie in the tranquil realm of eternal beauty and joy.

And yet one cannot rid himself of the oppressive sense
of something else in Nature, something dark and sinister.
What does it mean?

I

To a sensitive person, the suffering in the natural world
is painful, disturbing, sometimes appalling. He cannot
close his eyes to it. Everywhere he is confronted and
saddened by apparent waste, ruthlessness and cruelty.
Is this as great as it seems? Much depends upon one's
point of view and the scope of his vision. Alfred Wal-
lace, codiscoverer with Darwin of evolution, was more
impressed with the joyous side of Nature than with its
dark side, and one of the most sensitive and keenly ob-
servant of naturalists, John Muir, vigorously denied that
there is any dark side of Nature—at least among the
mountains that he loved. To him night, cold, tempest,
ice, flood, fire, decay, death, earthquake, all spelled Love.
The storm, he said, is Nature rocking the earth cradle;
in the earthquake she is trotting her children on her knee.
Criticizing Ruskin, Muir wrote: "I know something
about the blasted trunk and the barren rock, the moaning
of the bleak winds, the solemn solitudes of moors and

seas, the roar of the black, perilous, merciless whirlpools of the mountain streams; and they have a language for me, but they declare nothing of wrath or hell, only Love plain as was ever spoken." [1]

By contrast, that close comrade and annalist of the sea, Joseph Conrad, according to John Galsworthy, found no joy in the Great Deep. "Many might suppose," writes Galsworthy, "that Conrad would naturally settle by the sea. He never did. He had seen too much of it. . . . The sea was no friend of one too familiar with its moods. . . . His hero is not the sea, but man in conflict with that cruel and treacherous element. Ships he loved, but the sea—No." [2]

Do mountains and sea, then, tell conflicting tales? If not, who was right, Muir or Conrad? This, at last, may be said: The mountains are not desolate nor does the wind "moan," nor is the sea "cruel" or "treacherous." To find gloom or cruelty or treachery anywhere in Nature is to read human traits into the nonhuman. Nature cannot "smile and smile and be a villain"; only man is capable of that. Unless, perchance, there is an irresponsible Artist who creates without purpose or principle.

> This round of green, this orb of flame,
>   Fantastic beauty; such as lurks
>   In some wild Poet, as he works
>   Without a conscience or an aim.[3]

[1] *Life and Letters,* I, p. 378.
[2] "Reminiscences of Conrad," *Scribner's Magazine,* January, 1923, p. 7.
[3] *In Memoriam,* XXXIV.

There appears to be a growing disposition influencing even some theologians—if not to conceive of God as such a wild Poet, or Experimenter, at least to detach Him altogether from Nature, reduce Him to finiteness, and regard Him as an Ally of man, who is doing His best to help him against the force of a Blind Nature which is ruthlessly frustrating him at every point.[4]

II

It may be well to defer an attempt to determine whether Nature in effect, if not in intention, is dark and hostile or friendly and helpful, until we have glanced at two or three of the more pertinent conclusions which men have reached concerning the natural world in the long familiarities of contact with her, through the generations. These conclusions seem simple enough to the modern mind but they have been attained only after many years of severe experience and reflection.

The first is, that *events in the natural world are not the immediate acts of God*. It has taken a very long time to arrive at this now commonplace conclusion. In fact, it required a complete reversal of Everyman's initial ideas. Throughout the earlier stages of human thought, and well into the modern period, it was the common assumption that all the acts of Nature *are* acts of God, or the gods. Primitive man was not the only one who

[4] The idea of a finite God was greatly furthered by H. G. Wells in his *God the Invisible King*. For an admirable criticism of this conception see Bishop McConnell's: *Is God Limited?*

thought thus. Neither intellectual nor spiritual culture readily rose above the idea. The Greek tragedies attributed misfortune to the gods, or to Fate. The idea that God sends prosperity and adversity, according to His favor or disfavor, holds sway in a large part of the Old Testament and still rules the minds of many who have failed to read their Old Testament in the light of the New. It is reflected in many of the Psalms. It is the point of attack of that great drama of religious perplexity, the book of Job, where it receives, in one of its aspects, a telling blow. Against the common belief of his time that misfortune and accident, disaster and disease are evidences of the Divine displeasure Job indignantly protests. And yet, even in the midst of his passionate rejection of the charge that sin is the cause of his sufferings, he attributes his afflictions to the hand of God. "He breaketh me with breach upon breach; he runneth upon me like a giant." [5]

No true understanding of Nature and the disasters and diseases which befall men was possible until this idea was cast aside. It lingered on in the theology of the Church fathers and of the Middle Ages. Even the Reformation failed to remove it. Calvin held that every drop of rain falls by Divine *fiat*. Until the year 1787, when the Protestant Episcopal Church of America removed it from its Book of Common Prayer, the injunction of the priest remained, not "to kindle God's wrath" or "provoke Him

[5] Job 16:14.

to plague us with divers disease and sundry kinds of death."

Jesus challenged this whole assumption when he declared that the sun shines and the rain falls on evil and good alike, and again in his words regarding the fall of the tower of Siloam.[6] In the narrative of the healing of the man blind from birth (in the Fourth Gospel), the answer he returned to those who queried as to the cause of the blindness was: "Neither hath this man sinned nor his parents that he was born blind." It was the healing, rather than the blindness, that Jesus attributed to God.

It is only since the rise of modern science that men have come—and not all of them yet—to realize that natural laws do not represent God's intention toward them individually. Whatever the dark side of Nature means, it clearly does not mean the displeasure of God toward those who suffer from the operation of natural laws.

III

Another illuminating truth about Nature which has only of late found its way into human consciousness is that *natural objects as we know them are the result of a process of continuous evolution.* It has taken age-long observation and reflection to discover this. Indeed, only to our own and the preceding generation has it become

[6] This does not mean that Jesus detached the natural order from God. Indeed, he seems to have regarded it as expressive of the Divine Beneficence; only he refused to attribute the individual ills which accompany it to the Divine intention.

fully understood. A world in which evolution is at work
cannot be regarded as if it were one in which all things
were created as they now are. The dark and forbidding
must be judged as related to an evolving, and, in that
sense, still imperfect, whole.

The universal process of development involves a double
process of change—change in the parts in their several
stages of development, each genus, species, and individual
undergoing its own process of change—and change in the
whole as influenced, *e.g.,* by those climatic changes which
affect all forms of life.

The significance of this universal space-time evolutionary process is enormous. Within it are swept all
objects and forms of life, from the simplest to the most
highly organized. It carries the mind backward to remote and germinal beginnings and forward to an un-
imaginable outcome. Now is the universe a son of God
and it doth not yet appear what it shall be. The dark
side of Nature cannot be intelligently regarded except as
related to this vast, unceasing, evolutionary process whose
end is not yet.

A strange and bewildering planetary and biological
past precedes our era, full of curious and disproportion-
ate, as well as beautiful, forms. Palæontology is un-
earthing the skeletons of huge reptilian monsters for
whose existence we can see no possible reason. What
purpose can these

"Dragons of the prime
That tore each other in their slime"

have served?   What can the Creator have meant by allowing them a place in the evolutionary process?   Can it
be just because He is a God of love that He permitted
these clumsy and cruel actors to have their brief day in
the long course of upward moving life?   After all, the
most significant fact about these monsters is *that they
have become extinct*.   They had their day and ceased to
be.   In their places have ensued forms of life which
awaken unfailing interest and admiration.   When a
friend of mine asks me: Why dinosaurs? I reply: Why
are dinosaurs no more?   They were on the way to the
lark and the thrush.   Evolution seems to be constantly
saying: "What is the chaff to the wheat?   Watch my
working under the great Taskmaster's eye, and see how,
silently but surely, the unfit give place to the fit, the ugly
to the beautiful, the cruel to the gentle—so that the meek
are coming to inherit the earth!"   The outstanding fact
about Nature seems to be her constant improvement on
herself.   Dinosaurs and dinotheres and all their kind lie
buried in alluvial deposits.   Ice ages have fulfilled their
task and are gone, leaving rounded hills and charming
valleys and picturesque canyons, tenanted by marvelously
beautiful creatures of earth and air who, if they still
battle and devour also serve and coöperate.

Yet this is not all.   Consider the still greater beauty
and sublimity that may appear in the future!   For the
possibilities of further development in the evolutionary
process are beyond our power to imagine.   Am I re-
minded that this is irrelevant, because the scientist can

tell in advance what the future of this planet and all that inhabit it is to be—*i.e.*, a lifeless, frozen clod revolving in space in silent desolation?

Even if it were granted that this outcome is as certain as some scientists predict, still no one can say what transformations may not occur before that distant time arrives, partly through development taking place in Nature herself and partly through the transforming agencies and operations of developing man. Nature seems to have been waiting, as Paul said, for the coming of the sons of God, not only that she may be released from her own "bondage of corruption" but to help man on his way.[7] Human diseases of all forms are yielding to the skill of medical science. Suffering has been largely relieved and will become still more so. As for war, that darkest and most damnable of evils—man's own invention—what chance of survival has it before an awakened racial intelligence?

God, Nature, and Man together are making all things new. The future is full of promise for human progress and happiness. Yet all depends—ay, there's the rub— but the incentive, too—on men being true to their high calling and living as sons of God.

IV

This leads to still another aspect of Nature which is slowly coming to the fore, which relieves its darker side—

[7] Rom. 8:22.

the fact that not only man but every living organism apparently has a part in fashioning itself and finding its own way of subsistence. There are two conspiring factors in evolution: environment and reaction upon environment. So long as the first of these alone was recognized, Nature seemed a universal and in many respects terrible reign of determinism. But since the second factor came to light—reaction upon environment—organs and devices of destruction which were formerly regarded as the direct creations of God have taken a very different aspect. The serpent's venom—is it not its own device for self-defense and attack? The saber-tooth—is it not the tiger's own weapon, fashioned by the skill and might with which it is so fully endowed?

Every living species seems to have had to meet the life problem in its own way. And many and singular are the ways they have devised—some by flight and others by cunning, some by sheer might, and others by secreting poison, some by "digging in," and others, like the ants and bees, by wise, corporate living. By the latter method safety and sustenance have been successfully secured, although at the expense of individual development, to an astonishing degree.

It is to Schopenhauer that we are indebted for one of the earliest and clearest insights into this aspect of Nature. Full of discernment are these words of his:

We observe that many animals manifest the will to use organs which they do not yet possess. The goat and the ox butt before they have horns, the wild-boar attacks with that part of his snout where tusks are going to be, he does not, as might be done, fight with his teeth. . . . Hence the will is the principle of organization, the center of creative evolution. Wild beasts that desire to tear their prey to pieces, to live on plunder and on blood, have teeth and huge claws, strong muscles, piercing eyes; such, on the other hand, as, by instinct, do not desire to fight, but to seek safety in flight, develop, instead of organs of defense a fine sense of hearing, slender and agile legs. The porcupine, the hedgehog and the tortoise cover themselves with a shell because they do not desire to flee. The will plays the same part, although this is not so apparent, in the vegetable kingdom. Here, too, everything is striving, desire, unconscious appetition. The tree-top desiring light, invariably tends to assume a vertical position, unless it finds it elsewhere. The root which desires moisture often seeks for it in the most roundabout manner. . . . Hence, here as in the animal kingdom, everything is reduced to will, to that elementary will which we call irritability.[8]

"And God said to all creatures: *Increase and multiply,* differentiate, develop, vary, build up your own organisms in your own ways, search out your own methods of getting food, devise your own means of self-protection and propagation, make the earth a very laboratory for nourishing, protecting, and renewing life! [9] Run, fly, swim, leap, kill, feed, play, sing, fight, love, reproduce, nurture! Climb to heights of skill and strength and

[8] Weber, *History of Philosophy* (Revised Edition), p. 449.

[9] "The science of physics rests upon the postulate of determinism; the science of biology, unless it is to ignore deliberately the phenomenon of behavior, must abandon this postulate and substitute therefor a postulate of choice or freedom." Gilbert N. Lewis, *The Anatomy of Science,* p. 218.

beauty—until man comes. Lo! he is your interpreter, your lord, as well as your brother. He will abuse you, torment you, enslave you, ravage you, yet in the end help you to mount still higher in your ascent. He will admire you, cherish you, cultivate you, love you, refashion you. And he himself will go on climbing higher and higher, learning how to conquer and reconstruct his environment, using you, enjoying you, helped by you and helping you— until you all perish together as creatures of time and change and man goes on as inheritor of a new and higher life." Thus spake (as I heard in my dream) the Elohist.

In view of such discoveries as these—that Nature's acts are in accordance with law, that she is in process, and not to be judged as complete; and that the deeds and devices of her children are the outcome, in large part, of their own way of meeting the issue of their subsistence— Nature's dark side can hardly be regarded as contradicting the Fatherhood of God.

On the other hand, to account for Nature as independent of any Higher Power creates great difficulties. "The perfections of Nature," declared Pascal, "show that she is in the image of God, her defects show that she is only his image." Nature self-produced, or chance-produced, is far more difficult to conceive than Nature caused, endowed, given freedom—but directed.

It is possible, of course, to read the idea of unity and purpose out of the universe; but natural phenomena conform too clearly to concepts of law and order to justify regarding them as a jumble or even as a mere aggregate.

What will account, for example, for animal instinct, whose achievements in insect life, as they have been pictured by J. H. Fabre, are so remarkable as to lead Bergson to regard instinct as more wonderful than human intellect? What will explain the prescience by which the mother insect knows just where to lay her eggs and the new-born larva knows just how to select its food? How does the unerring bee know the way home to the hive? Granted that the singularly intricate and subtle methods by which life is sustained and propagated, especially among the anthropoids, may have been built up through countless generations, what explains the initial endowment of potential sagacity by which these tiny organisms have worked out their astonishing adaptations to life? One cannot glance into the insect world through the eyes of such an observer as Fabre without being struck by "the amazing essays of passion and variety with which the universal law which rules the transmission of life is evolved." [10]   Whence is this passionate, indomitable, progressive *nisus* we call *life?* If life sprang out of the inorganic, what gave it impetus, momentum, the will to live, to transmit itself, and to protect its progeny? Is it a blind urge? Why, then, does it push on toward intelligence, affection, altruism? If it is emergent, from what or Whom does it ultimately emerge? Such questions all lead back to a hidden root. Is God here? So it seemed to Fabre. He could not have more astonished his visitor,

[10] C. V. Legros, *Fabre, Poet of Science*, p. 128.

the Curé, than by saying to him as he did: "I do not *believe* in God; but I see Him."[11]

The most reasonable solution of the problem of Nature seems to be to regard the natural world as the progressive creation of a purposive, benevolent Intelligence who has infilled it with an inexhaustible developing potency, intelligence, and germinal freedom which enable all the various life-forms to work out, each for itself, its unique self-expression, yet who holds all within the bounds of an all-comprehending unity and a progressive purpose. No one has stated this more positively, or with a better basis of scientific knowledge, than Professor J. Arthur Thompson, who says:

We have sought to envisage the variety of life—hundreds of thousands of distinct individualities or species; the abundance of life—like a river always tending to overflow its banks; the diffusion of life—exploring and exploiting every corner of land and sea; the insurgence of life—self-assertive, persistent, defiant, continually achieving the apparently impossible; the cyclical development of life—ever passing from birth, through love, to death; the intricacy of life—every cell a microcosm; the subtlety of life—every drop of blood an index of idiosyncrasies; the inter-relatedness of life—with myriad threads woven in a patterned web; the drama of life—plot within plot, age after age, with every conceivable illustration of the twin motives of hunger and love; the flux of life—even under our short-lived eyes; the progress of life—slowly creeping up-

[11] "J. H. Fabre at Home," *The Living Age,* February 9, 1924. "A naturalistic Explanation [of instinct], while it is an alternative to the notion that instinct was a miracle of creation, is quite compatible with the idea that it is a marvel of providence." W. P. Paterson, *The Nature of Religion,* The Gifford Lectures of 1924 and 1925, p. 105.

wards through unthinkable time, expressing itself in ever
nobler forms, the beauty of life—every finished organism an
artistic harmony; the morality of life—spending itself to the
death for other than individual ends; the mentality of life—
sometimes quietly dreaming, sometimes sleep-walking, sometimes widely awake; and the victory of life—subduing material things to its will, and in its highest reaches controlling
itself towards an increasing purpose. [We thus reach the]
provisional conclusion [that] individualities with mind, with
freedom, and with purpose cannot be accounted for in terms
of a ground of reality without mind, without freedom, without
purpose.[12]

All forms of life may thus, perhaps, be regarded, by
virtue of coöperant creation, as at once Nature's and
God's; each beauty of flower and bird and insect its own,
yet His; all varieties of organism and adaptation to environment self-evolved being endowed with potency to
develop parasitic, ugly and degenerate forms (human
mixture thus mirrored in nature) by the misuse of freedom. One sometimes wonders if (as a friend of mine
has suggested) diseased growths, like cancer and all forms
of malignant parasitism, may not be due to rebel colonies,
seeking to thrive at the expense of a higher organism.

But *is* this *creation?* In the sense of mechanical, "car-
penter" creation, No; in the sense of originating and
directive creation, Yes. "He was good," says Plato of
the Creator in the *Timæus,* "and therefore He grudged
existence to nothing." It might not be far wrong to ex-
tend the discerning word of Paul to Christians to the

[12] J. Arthur Thomson, *The System of Animate Nature.*

whole animate creation, as if the Divine word had said to each living organism: "Work out your own salvation with fear and trembling, for it is God that worketh in you both to will and to do of his good pleasure."

V

Thus we return to the question of the dark side of Nature, with which we started, with at least a tentative answer. The dark side may be reasonably regarded as subordinate, possibly inevitable. Viewed in the light of an evolutionary process which requires freedom, whose products are more and more admirable and whose outcome is personality, it loses much of its somberness. John Muir seems to have been, on the whole, in the right of it, oblivious though he may have been to developmental imperfections, primal darknesses, and remaining ills. The bright side of Nature, we may reasonably accept as the chief side—life, enjoyment, beauty, development—and the dark side the accompaniment and by-product, as nearly as we can judge, of that ever increasing autonomy without which life would be mechanism, not life, mind behavior, not mind, and men and women *automata,* and not persons.

If the process of evolution means anything worth concerning ourselves with, its only significance consists in the fact that, however low down in the scale of creation man started, and however silly, childish, cruel and mean he has shown himself in his course upwards, yet, at the uppermost point in this process, real persons have appeared, fine and full, and high and beautiful in their integrity. If only one person had appeared, giving the promise of the eventual coming of others, and the final ripening of all the fruit on the life tree of the world, would not the travail of the ages be abundantly justified? No tiny insect that had its part in the infinite drama would have then lived, and suffered, and shone in the sunshine in vain! [13]

In some such sense, in the fusion of all life in an ascending flame toward its culmination in the person, and then receiving from him a kind of recreation, may there not be meaning in that extravagant but strangely appealing word from a Buddhist text: "Then shall it be accomplished that no living thing, no particle of dust, shall fail to attain unto Buddhahood." [14]

[13] Charles F. Dole, "Is God Personal?" *Unity*, September 7, 1925.
[14] *Avatemasaka Sutra*.

CHAPTER X

The Problem of Suffering and Death

The unwarranted Dramatization of Struggle and Pain in Animal Life—
Man the Cause of the greatest Animal Suffering—The Influence of Religion in mitigating Animal Suffering; Jainism and Christianity compared
—Human Suffering, its Nature and Values—Suffering in its Effect upon
the Development of Character—Death in relation to enlarged and enhanced Life; the Sex Instinct and the Renewal of Life—Personal Immortality needed to carry Life to its Completion—Divine Suffering, like
Divine Joy, vicarious, sympathetic, and all-embracing.

IF THIS is God's world, why should it be so marred
and seamed by suffering and death? It is a hoary
and poignant enigma. "Facts," said Robert Burns, "are
chiels that winna ding." Suffering and death are irre-
pressible facts. We have no right to turn away from
them.[1] Neither are we obliged to take them at their face
value.

I

Since the rise of Darwinism, emphasis has lain upon
the struggle and pain in nature. The forward look of

[1] This chapter continues the discussion of "Natural Evil" commenced
in Chapter IX, taking up some of the problems there touched upon and
carrying them on into the life of man as far as he is a part of nature.

evolution inspires hope; but its backward look has left sensitive minds shocked by the strife and pain of the life of their fellow creatures. No longer is it possible to look at Nature through rose-colored glasses. An easy-going optimism toward nature is as insubstantial as an easy-going optimism regarding humanity.

And yet the very common impression that nature is nothing but a field of carnage and a scene of shame is wholly unjustified. The "struggle for existence" has been grossly exaggerated. John Fiske, e.g., in his striking and graphic picture of a summer field, described its life as one of "unceasing toil, of crowding and jostling, where the weaker fall unpitied by the way, of starvation from hunger and cold, of robbery utterly shameless and murder utterly cruel." [2] Science does not bear out this representation. This is to draw upon imagination as much as to picture the scene as one all of peace and happiness.[3] It was not without pertinence that Alexander Pope wrote: "All nature's difference keeps all nature's peace." The principle of coöperation is quite as potent as that of competition, as Prince Kropotkin pointed out. Symbiosis is appearing everywhere. Whoever has considered the facts of chemical attraction, or the orderly movement of electrons, or has watched a bee pollenizing a flower, or a pair of birds building a nest, or a city building a water supply

[2] *Through Nature to God,* p. 63.

[3] John Stuart Mill in his arraignment of nature in his *Essay on Nature* is guilty of the same kind of exaggeration. Many less earnest writers have followed in this vein.

or a hospital, knows that it is *coöperation* that keeps the whole world going.

The darkest page in the story of animal suffering is that which man himself has imposed upon his brothers, big and little, of earth and air and water. This has been due in part to an inhuman cruelty such as the animals themselves cannot rival; in part to a callousness which is unable or unwilling to feel the suffering which it inflicts; but chiefly to a love of "sport" which delights to engage in or to watch a trial of animal strength and skill. Bear baiting, cock fighting, bull fighting, cruel methods of hunting and trapping, not to say fishing—some of them obsolete, others still practiced—are sorry forms of a love of sport which is not intentionally cruel yet allows itself to fall into savage barbarity and cruelty.

II

Religion, in conjunction with moral sentiment, has banished the worst forms of cruelty to animals, but has not put an end to it. In contrast with other religions—especially Jainism, Buddhism, and Mohammedanism—Christianity has failed to do its full part in this respect. Yet this is not because feeling for living things is wanting in it. One can discern a deep tenderness in Jesus' words regarding animals and birds. The truest of his followers have shared this feeling. Who had more of it than St. Francis? How attractive are the tales of the friendliness of the Christian hermits toward beasts and birds! [4] Feeling for the pain of animals is not wanting in English literature. Shakespeare's picture of the wounded deer in the Forest of Arden is witness of his sympathy for animal suffering. Cowper was a true friend of animals and alleviator of their sufferings. Burns' "Poor Mailie" and "To a Mouse" cannot be forgotten. Nor has active work for protection and relief been wanting. Societies for the prevention of cruelty to animals have proven themselves truly Christian organizations.

Yet consideration for animals has not characterized Christian peoples as a whole. We stand condemned in this respect before religions which are regarded as inferior. Jainism in India—going back to the sixth century B.C. and still numbering over a million adherents—has as one of its chief tenets a prohibition against killing any living thing, great or small. Poisonous snakes, harmful insects, loathsome vermin, destructive animals, all are protected by this sacred pact of nondestruction. This humane attitude is worthy of honor; and yet its entire lack of perspective and sense of values renders it singularly unbalanced and unreasonable. It transfers suffering in many cases from the lowest forms of animal life to man and multiplies manifold the total amount of real distress. For it is blind to two important facts—the want of a highly developed nervous organism in many forms of animal life which makes their suffering comparatively

[4] These are delightfully narrated in *The Book of Saints and Friendly Beasts* by Abbie Farwell Brown.

light, and the recognition of graded values, which renders a certain amount of sacrifice of animal to human life both reasonable and right. As contrasted with this lack of perspective, Christendom has kept a clear head, if not always a feeling heart. Jesus' word, "How much is a man better than a sheep!" involves the principle of a reasonable subordination of the animal world to human uses—even including vivisection, humanely practiced—but not the thoughtless and heartless imposition of suffering (in trapping game, for instance) which is still so great a shame to Christian peoples. When we have learned to remove the needless load of pain which we have imposed upon the animal world, it will be more pertinent to dwell upon the suffering which living creatures inflict upon each other as a defect in the world order.

III

When one comes to the problem of *human* suffering, he may well walk softly and speak hesitantly. No one who has suffered acutely will attempt to minimize the reality, intensity and mystery of physical pain. Yet there are two or three considerations which ought not to be forgotten.

The first is, that an organism so responsive to sensation as the human body, so sensitive to the exquisite pleasure which accompanies the normal functioning of the senses, must, it would seem, by reason of its very responsiveness, also be sensitive to pain. Moreover, if pleasure is a reassuring sign of physical well-being, pain is a danger signal of physical ill-being and, as such, serves the interests of the body. It would, of course, be extravagant to claim that this fact disposes of the whole problem of pain, or that the degree of pain is never greater than it need be in order to impel to action for relief. It is not impossible to imagine human bodies impervious to disease and injury and then to find fault with our present bodies because they are not thus immune; but such objections incline to be captious. Wrong, uncleanly, unwholesome living is responsible for most of human ills. Diseases of uncivilized life—plague and pestilence—give place to diseases of "civilized" life; testifying, for the most part, to wrong habits and conditions of living. For these, *man* is in the main responsible. According to plain reasoning, it seems by no means strange that the human organism, whose regular functions are attended with keen, continuous and varied pleasure, should, by reason of that very capacity, be subject to pain, due to injury and disease.

Another footnote to the problem of human pain is the fact that as, under the increasing abuses of "civilized" life, the nervous system has grown more sensitive, increasing means for the relief of pain have been discovered. Who that has gained relief from pain through the administration of an anesthetic has not felt a deep sense of gratitude? It is an illustration of the need of constant readjustment between physical and moral forces that with the use of these subtle and powerful drugs there has come a new and acute moral danger, calling for both self-control and social control to prevent their abuse. For a powerful drug, like a sharp instrument, cannot be expected to be harmless when it is misused.[5]

IV

Yet by far the greatest light upon the problem of pain comes from its effect upon the training of character. To recognize this is not to deny the deadening effect upon the inner life which pain sometimes has, nor the fact that physical disease often blunts the moral sense. It would be foolish to cloak these facts. Yet, with all this in view, who of us, looking back over his own experience, would not say that the illnesses through which he has passed and the sufferings which he has undergone, both for himself and for others, have been for his real betterment? They have admitted him to "the Fellowship of Pain," as Dr. Schweitzer has called it, and have in most cases helped to make more of a man of him.

[5] Nothing could be more hideous, or a greater reproach to the laxity of the enforcement of our laws, than the increase of the narcotic drug addiction, as it was brought out in a speech in the House of Representatives, February 18, 1925, by Hon. Walter F. Lineberger, from which I take the following: "Narcotic drug addiction is a serious universal problem which has become acute in America through the spread of heroin addiction. There are probably five times as many narcotic drug addicts in the world as there were ever slaves at any one time, and the bondage is far more abject and far more dangerous. America is being assailed by opium with Asia as a base, by heroin and synthetic drugs with Europe as a base. An unscrupulous traffic within joins the traffic from without."

If the opportunity were in one's power to eliminate pain and sickness from human life altogether—looking at the matter from the point of view of the good of humanity as a whole—who would dare to say: "Let pain, illness, privation, discomfort in every form, cease from this moment, with all that goes with them—the strength of endurance, the moral discipline, the ministries for relief, the sympathy and service which they awaken"? What would supply the place of these in the education of character? We are fond of quoting, in disappointed or superficial moments, the well-known lines from the *Rubaiyat*:

> Ah Love! could thou and I with Fate conspire
> To grasp this sorry Scheme of Things entire,
> Would we not shatter it to bits—and then
> Re-mould it nearer to the Heart's Desire!

But if we should remold it to the heart's desire, minus suffering, misfortune, and every other ill, what sort of men and women would emerge? Poor, pampered, soft creatures, it is to be feared, with neither strength of character nor sympathy.

No one would be so bold as to say that such considerations as these explain away the problem of human suffering, but they reduce its proportions and take some of the sting out of its intensity.

V

Turning now from Pain to her dread sister, Death, what can be said toward lessening the sinister shadow cast by this apparent contradiction of the Fatherhood of God? There is no cloaking the imperious fact of death, its inevitableness, its incalculable weight of defeat and sorrow. Perhaps no piece of literature has pictured the universal reign of death more graphically than the well-known poem of the youthful Bryant, a poem which itself will never die, although its pathos and melancholy betray the immature hand. The trouble with *Thanatopsis* is that it emphasizes, not to say celebrates, the lesser of two obverse facts. Death is mighty, ubiquitous, all-consuming, but it is only an adjunct, an attendant, a servant, perchance of the greater reality—Life. Francis Thompson sounded a note that is needed to offset Bryant, when in his *Easter Day* he wrote:

> All dies,
> But all is born.

The fact which Newman Smyth brought out so cogently in *The Place of Death in Evolution* and later in *Constructive Natural Theology*—i.e., that Death works "for the further differentiation and enrichment of life," [6] is as cogent as it is neglected. Death seems all-devouring; yet as it sweeps away myriads of insects, billions of birds and animals, and countless generations of men, it thereby makes room for so many more to take their places. Thus the cup of life is kept brimming over, fed by perpetual springs.

[6] *Constructive Natural Theology*, p. 20.
"Death is as much a part of the plan as birth is; and who knows which is the better of the two?" Sir Henry Jones.

Lavish Life! how it pours the wealth of its abundance into the meadows of God, like a mighty stream that knows no spending! Death tries in vain to stay the vital flood, but itself is "swallowed up" of life. Reproduction triumphs over dissolution. The greater the number death sweeps away, the greater the sum total of lives. The process results in multiplying indefinitely the number of individuals who repeat the life story, or sing the life lyric, each in its own strain and with a zest of its own.

The lover of Nature, who season after season watches the successive ranks of the wild flowers come and go, experiences constant wonder and delight at the way these gentle children of the fields and woods succeed one another. With what fine chivalry, so to speak, do they make room for each other—hepaticas, violets, cowslips, trilliums, laurels, lilies, roses, gentians, godetias, asters, and the rest—successively making way for the next group, as if with a gracious *morituri salutamus*. If we are to dramatize the life of the vegetable kingdom surely this pleasant fancy is as true to nature as to paint in startling colors its fierce conflicts for light and air and soil.

Thou perceivest the flowers put forth their precious odours;
And none can tell how from so small a centre comes such sweet,
Forgetting that within the centre Eternity expands
   Its ever-during doors.[7]

Nor may we be blind to the part which the *sex instinct* plays in the renewal of life. After leaving the lowest forms of life, which reproduce by division, the mutual

[7] William Blake, *Jerusalem*.

attraction of sex enters and grows ever more eager and glad. With what fascination and delight—far-heard music and varied romance—does this invest the upward pathway of life! Quite pure and joyous it all is—in spite of the bravery and battle attending "natural selection"— until it reaches its culmination, where, unhappily, it is too wont to yield to dishonor and degradation, in human sex relationship. Is there no indication of Supreme Benefi- cence behind the impetuous, creative, songful renewal of life? One may find in it the mere foison and fecundity of lustful instinct, generating, begetting, multiplying, without meaning or purpose; or he may see in it one ex- pression, however remote from its source, of Universal Love. Aristotle revealed his insight when he wrote: "For it is the most natural function in all living things . . . to reproduce their species; animal producing animal and plant plant, *in order that they may, so far as they can, share in the eternal and the divine.*" [8] According to one's own mind will be his world, either one in which "there always, always something sings" a song of love and joy, or a lewd and senseless roundelay of the primal and unholy lust of life.

VI

Yet this constant victory of life, this leading of cap- tivity captive, this service of death to birth, would seem to fail of an adequate and worthy outcome if, when the individual person emerges, tastes of the wonder and

[8] *De Anima* II, 4 (Italics are mine).

beauty of the world, is ripened by the discipline of suffering and moral achievement, and has begun to win a personality of his own, he suddenly falls into emptiness and oblivion. If, after all this preparative discipline, the supreme product of nature and supernature, acme and judge of values, is swiftly and finally cut off by so inferior a foe as death, the ruthlessness of the outcome would go far to discredit the whole process.

"Surplus of nature's dread activity

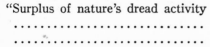

Thou hast no reason why! Thou canst have none:
Thy being's being is contradiction."

Here, it would seem, is the acid test, the crux of the whole life drama: Does it issue in personal immortality? Without this possibility, the one self-conscious observer of the universe within it, surveying it with intelligent eye, might pronounce it all purposeless, incomprehensible, self-defeating.[9] Yet who can *know* that this is not the outcome? Well, it is not ours to *know,* but to live in the light of the ennobling and rational *hope* of the perdurance of personality.

VII

One more aspect of the problem of suffering requires at least a word. Nature suffers, man suffers. Does God suffer?

[9] "Souls, if they are worth the making are worth the keeping, and the universe would fail in its duty if it did not preserve them." John Laird, *The Idea of the Soul,* p. 186.

It is impossible to answer this question, if God is our Father, otherwise than in the affirmative—as Jesus answered it. Yet Divine Suffering must needs be of a kind which none but He can have, that of pure sympathy. No suffering for Himself—due, as with us, to an imperfect nature, implicating Him in the exigencies of a developing order—but all for others, all, that is, *vicarious* suffering. This makes the Divine suffering immeasurably greater than ours in extent and immeasurably less in kind, greater because all-embracing, all-comprehending, all-compassionate; less because aware, as we cannot be, of the relation of suffering to the end it serves.

It is possible for us to understand something of what Divine suffering must be through our own developing experience. As one advances in personality, and grows more sympathetic, wider visioned, more altruistic, his suffering becomes less and less "personal," *i.e.*, self-centered (how inadequate are our terms!) and more and more vicarious. The sufferings of one's kin, his associates, his neighbors, his community, his country, the world—so far as he can enter into them—become in some slight measure his own. Into the chalice of his happiness fall countless drops of bitterness for the woes of others and he drinks them, knowing that in so far as his suffering is unselfish it is like that of God.

Yet we may not stop here. There is another side of our experience, also, that suggests something of what God's inconceivably larger experience may be. The more one advances in personality, the richer, deeper, more

pervasive becomes his *joy* and also the more *vicarious*.
It expands to embrace all of nature, to share in the life
of every flower that blooms by the wayside, every insect
that flits across his path in the sunshine, every bird whose
song floats across the fields to his ear. He comes to feel,
with Wordsworth,

> . . . "the sentiment of Being, spread
> O'er all that moves and all that seemeth still;
> O'er all that, lost beyond the reach of thought
> And human knowledge, to the human eye
> Invisible, yet liveth to the heart." [10]

Yet these are but the narrower ranges of vicarious joy.
It goes out, with fuller and more understanding sympathy, to share the common human joys: the joy of children
at play, youth rejoicing in the mystery and music of life,
strong men and women exulting in their work, the quiet-
ness and peace of the aged; the joy of creative work, of
art, of thought, of worship.

Thus, in infinitely greater degree, we may conceive it
to be with the All-Father—suffering vicariously with his
creatures, and especially with men, as they suffer, sorrow,
sin, and die; yet also rejoicing with them, with a joy
that exceeds the sorrow, as they delight in existence, as
they love, as they achieve, as they pass from life to life.
And this, not because His experience is identical with our
experience, as Monism holds, but rather because His experience is cognizant and appreciative of ours, as the
father shares, more understandingly than the child can

[10] *The Prelude,* Book First.

possibly realize, his limited experience.[11] "I sometimes think one might conceive of God," wrote Nettleship, "as a being who might experience what we call the intensest pain and pleasure, without being affected by it—*who made everything his own without becoming any of it.*"

[11] For a striking presentation of the kind of knowledge we may think of as possessed by Deity, the reader may be referred to a volume published since the above was written, under the title *The Nature of Deity*, by J. E. Turner (especially pp. 61 ff.).

CHAPTER XI

The Problem of History

History presents puzzling Contrasts, yet certain reassuring Principles are seen to run through it—Purposefulness traceable in History—Moral Law as it influences the historic Process—Progress, though now widely questioned, revealed by History—The Possibility of a Philosophy of History complicated by the destructive Effects of Time; yet Time is also preservative and fructifying—Is a Key to History afforded by the Christian Revelation?—History a Drama which only the Fifth Act can completely illumine.

I

IF GOD is in truth the Father of men it is reasonable to expect that this fact will illumine human history with a light not too dim to be perceptible. Yet, when one looks into the record of the fraction of recorded human events and experiences which passes for history, it is difficult at first to discover much besides chaos. Races arising, migrating, warring, enslaving one another; nations coming to consciousness, struggling for power, lapsing into decay; great disasters—flood, famine, pestilence —sweeping away whole peoples; abortive struggles for liberty, winning a measure of success only to be whelmed

157

under some new form of tyranny; war dominating all, with its damnable cruelties and horrors, entailing suffering upon the innocent, furnishing spoil for the strong, stultifying all human values.

Yet this is only one side of the picture. The other side presents a very different aspect, showing progressive peoples making steady gains, moving forward in agriculture, industry, the arts, education, religion; in time of war displaying courage and endurance, and in the intervals of peace building homes and establishing beneficent educational, political, and social institutions.

These contrasted lights and shadows render the problem of history extremely difficult; yet not hopeless. For out of all the chaotic maelstrom of events—conquests, calamities, adventures, crimes, crusades, tragedies, inhumanities, losses, advances, lapses—emerge certain tendencies whose significance cannot be overlooked. They may be roughly described as indications of *purposefulness,* of *moral law,* and of *progress.* If these are verifiable, we may say, with Carlyle, that "in the wondrous, boundless jostle of things (an aimful *Power* presiding over it, say rather, dwelling *in* it), a result comes out that may be put-up with." [1]

---

[1] *On History Again.* Perhaps it is possible to go further than the discerning but doughty seer of Chelsea and find a result not only to be "put-up with" but fraught with possibilities of undreamt-of good.

II

Whatever it may fail to disclose, history reveals an increasing complexity, differentiation, and organization of human interests and activities.

Both in nature and in human history there is constant change, movement, readjustment. The very restlessness of racial movements seems to have a meaning. Races early began to migrate. Why? It is not enough to say that they sought better living conditions. There was also an element of risk, of adventure, of faith even, in such migrations, the stirring of an impulse which cannot be explained merely in terms of the preservation of life. "Mankind has wandered from the trees to the plains, from the plains to the seacoast, from climate to climate, from continent to continent, and from habit of life to habit of life. When man ceases to wander he will cease to ascend in the scale of being. Physical wandering is still important, but greater still is the power of man's spiritual adventures—adventures of thought, adventures of passionate feeling, adventures of æsthetic experience." [2]

To trace in the migration of races, the rise and fall of empires and of nations, and in the emergence of higher types of civilization, the working out of a hard and fast "Divine plan" is to naïvely oversimplify the vast complexities of history. Yet it is difficult to eliminate the suggestion of purposefulness.

[2] A. N. Whitehead, *Science and the Modern World*, p. 290.

III

Moral law, too, asserts itself with increasing clearness as a determining factor in shaping history. Froude has stated this with a confidence that ignores the historian's customary caution: "One lesson, and only one, history may be said to repeat with distinctness; that the world is built somehow on moral foundations." [3] Von Ranke attributes such an insight to Thucydides, declaring that "the real advance made by Thucydides consists perhaps in this, that he perceived the motive forces of human history to be in the moral constitution of human nature." [4]

It would be an exaggeration to say that moral causes alone have determined the rise and fall of races and nations. Physical and mental superiority, combined with the advantages of natural and social environment, have been important factors. Yet along with natural resources and physical and mental advantages, have gone—as a necessary condition of advance—industry, social solidarity, a measure, at least, of right living. And these virtues, integrities, reliabilities, alone have made civilization possible. "Obscurely and slowly, yet visibly and measurably, moral influences in human affairs have become stronger and more widely extended than material influences." [5]

[3] *Short Studies on Great Subjects.*
[4] Quoted by P. V. N. Myers in *History as Past Ethics,* p. vii.
[5] Edward P. Cheney, "Law in History," *American Historical Review,* quoted by F. E. Teggert, *Theory of History,* p. 205.

Where moral integrity has failed, it is the dramatic lesson of history that decay and downfall have followed. Babylon, Assyria, Egypt, Greece, Rome—the story is no mere subject for schoolboy declamations, but is written deep, "with a pen of iron," for all generations to read. "The really constructive and regulative forces in history are in truth moral ideas and convictions." [6]

IV

Another ray of light breaks through the darkness of history in the emergence of *progress*. That there is progress—halting, irregular, accompanied by many lapses, but on the whole unmistakable—is the conviction of the average reader of history and, sometimes, even the conclusion of the historian. At least such was the case before the Great War. Since that time the question whether humanity really shows progress has been discussed with varying judgments. Dean Inge is skeptical of progress, and in his Romanes Lecture of 1920 on *The Idea of Progress* has cautioned against too generous an indulgence of the "superstition of progress": "Spiritual progress must be within the sphere of a reality which is not itself progressing." "We have no millennium to look forward to; but neither need we fear any protracted or widespread retrogression." [7]

[6] Myers, *Op. cit.*, p. 3.
[7] *Outspoken Essays,* Second Series. Cf. J. W. Buckham, "The Christian Platonism of Dean Inge," *The Journal of Religion,* January, 1924.

J. B. Bury in his *The Idea of Progress,* after a studious history of the idea as such, leaves its validity to individual faith: "The idea of the Progress of humanity belongs to the same order of ideas as Providence or personal immortality. It is true or it is false, and like them it cannot be proved either true or false. Belief in it is an act of faith."

L. P. Jacks dwells pertinently on the difficulties and dangers of a world not easily reducible to tameness and ease: "We have abandoned the hope, fervently entertained in our youth, that by due solution of 'world problems' the 'world' would one day be changed from difficult to easy, from dangerous to safe; and it is only when cowardice overcomes us (alas, not infrequently) that we wish it otherwise. For the Higher Powers in ordaining this dangerous existence for man did not forget to equip him with the qualities (now greatly weakened by his follies) that are needed for facing it." [8]

Ernst Troeltsch, with characteristic sincerity and reserve, sees relative progress but refers its completion to a world lying beyond the pale of history.

. . . A radical and absolute solution does not exist; there are only working, partial, synthetically uniting solutions. Yet the stream of life is always surging upward and onward. History within itself cannot be transcended, and knows of no salvation except in the form of devout anticipations of the Hereafter, or glorified transfigurations of partial salvations. The Kingdom of God and Nirvana lie outside all history. In history itself there are only relative victories; and these rela-

[8] "World Mending," *The Yale Review,* October, 1925, p. 11.

tive victories themselves vary greatly in power and depth, according to time and circumstance.[9]

Grant Showerman in a recent vivacious discussion of the subject points out that progress is not to be measured in terms of wealth, prosperity, machinery, prowess. It is something far deeper than that. Two men meet, after a discussion on the subject of progress, and one remarks to the other:

"You can talk all you want to about your steam and electricity and gasoline, and your easy communication and rapid transportation, and your organization and standardization," he said, "and even your schools and hospitals. No one of them, nor the whole lot of them together, necessarily means or insures progress. Progress is a matter of feeling; it is concerned with the emotional life of men. It is an affair of the spirit *and* the letter, but the essential one of the two is the spirit. Civilization is not so much a business as it is an art and a religion." [10]

These varied comments on progress are manifestly qualifications rather than denials of it.

V

The problem of history leads to that venturesome and absorbing enterprise, the Philosophy of History. Can there be a philosophy of history?

[9] *Christian Thought*, pp. 128-129.

[10] *University of California Chronicle*, Vol. XXVI, No. 3, p. 244. Professor Conklin writes similarly: "Human progress depends upon the increase and diffusion among men of both knowledge and ethics, reality and ideality, science and religion."

As if to block the possibility of any permanent constructive values in human life, and thus to thwart any attempt at a philosophy of history, there looms the figure of the great Destroyer. Time, crumbling man's works to dust, snatching the workman from his task at the moment when he is nearing accomplishment, carrying all men away "like a sleep," and by its perpetual robbery and devastation makes all human advance seem a mockery. The pathos of the destructive work of "Time" no one— as Professor Palmer has pointed out—has depicted with more intensity of feeling than Shakespeare.[11] Sonnet LXV sounds a note which is heard again and again, not only in the sonnets but in the plays:

> "Since brass, nor stone, nor earth, nor boundless sea
> But sad mortality o'ersways their power,
> How with this rage shall beauty hold a plea,
> Whose action is no stronger than a flower?
> O, how shall summer's honey breath hold out
> Against the wreckful siege of battering days,
> When rocks impregnable are not so stout,
> Nor gates of steel so strong, but time decays?
> O fearful meditation! where, alack!
> Shall Time's best jewel from Time's chest be hid?
> Or what strong hand can hold his swift foot back?
> Or who his spoil of beauty can forbid?
> O none, unless this miracle have might,
> That in black ink my love may still shine bright."

The miracle of ink, in the hands of such as Shakespeare,

[11] G. H. Palmer, *Intimations of Immortality in the Sonnets of Shakespeare.*

has had great "might", little of Time's ravages as it
has succeeded in arresting.

On the other hand, Time is also the great Fulfiller,
nourishing the seeds planted by man, and developing and
ripening them through long periods of growth, giving to
his creations in art, science, literature, even music (whose
very substance consists of fleeting sound), the crown of
full fruition, so that Emerson could write with measur-
able truth:

> "One accent of the Holy Ghost
> A heedless world has never lost."

Time with one hand, so to speak, ruthlessly demol-
ishes the products of human workmanship, and with the
other reshapes, protects, defends the results of human
effort, building about them granite walls of security so
that they survive all shock and change. Which of these
offices is the more significant? Is Time our Friend or
our Foe? Is "the wreckful siege of battering days" or
the "miracle of ink"—and other conservers of the past
from oblivion—the greater fact?

Surely one who is living in our present civilization,
built upon the achievements of the ages of stone and
iron, upon Greek art and philosophy, Roman law, and
Hebrew and Christian religion, heir of the ages, inheritor of all the past, cannot answer this question in purely
pessimistic terms.

VI

Is there, within history itself, any clear and conspicuous instance of Divine guidance, any series of events so striking and significant as to furnish a clue to the whole? If so, it may serve as a *pou sto* for constructing a philosophy of history.

The conviction that there is such a clue has arisen, with deep impressiveness, in connection with the life and mission of Jesus Christ and the consequences which have followed from it. The sense of something of unique import connected with Christ has held possession of thoughtful minds for twenty centuries. It came home with constantly deepening force to those who felt the immediate touch of his personality and to those who came to share its impress through them. Paul expressed it with commanding assurance in the first chapter of his epistle to the Colossians and concentrated it in the saying: "God was in Christ reconciling the world unto himself." It finds expression in the prologue of the Fourth Gospel and in a thousand successive philosophic and literary forms. It became crystallized in the term *revelation*. Browning voiced it thus:

"Then stand before that fact, that Life and Death,
Stay there at gaze, till it dispart, dispread,
As though a star should open out, all sides,
Grow the world on you, as it is my world."

Revelation is a daring conception, too bold for the

average historian even to consider. And yet it has exercised a profound influence upon the whole conception of history. In the form of the idea of a *Kingdom of God* it has incorporated itself into the very tissue of Occidental idealism. The idea of progress is intimately associated with it. It has entered into most of the Utopias, the social dreams, the hard-won victories, the forward movements, that have taken place in Christendom and has leavened the thought and ideals of humanity at large. Indeed the very idea of a philosophy of history is itself a Christian product.[12] Almost every philosophy of history, however extensive or meager—from Paul's *Epistle to the Romans* and Augustine's *City of God* to Lessing's *Education of the Human Race* and Hegel's *Lectures on the Philosophy of History*—has, either implicitly or explicitly, been based upon Christianity as a revelation of the deeper meaning of history. An adequate, not to say comprehensive, philosophy of history has not yet appeared, but an adequate organizing *principle* for it has been gained. That principle on the divine side appears as *revelation,* on the human side as *education.* The idea of history as a prolonged educative process has won increasing influence, although it is an education intense in its severity (perhaps necessarily), incomprehensible in many of its aspects, and as yet far from completion.

[12] "From the first Christianity had a philosophy of history." Article, "History," *Encyclopædia Britannica*, p. 529.

VII

In the long process of cosmic and human development certain races, generations, individuals, seem to be swallowed up in failure, calamity, obscurity, while others are lifted to heights of conspicuous fortune, success or significance. These contrasted fortunes are only partially traceable to moral desert. Why, then, should they happen? Apparently they are inseparable from the historic process itself, due to the solidarity, the freedom, and the unavoidable fortuities of human life. Jesus evidently pondered deeply the inequalities of his fellows and looked to the future for their solution: "Many that are first shall be last and the last first." "Blessed are ye that hunger now: for ye shall be filled. Blessed are ye that weep now: for ye shall laugh. . . . Woe unto you, that are full now! for ye shall hunger. Woe unto you, that laugh now! for ye shall mourn and weep." [13]   Is this the empty dream of a devout humanitarian and idealist; or insight into the true issues of human life and destiny?

History is a drama of which we may still be but in the first, or second act. Who can say what revelations and reversals, what restorations and consummations, the Fifth Act may not disclose—if, as Christianity holds, history consists not merely of temporal incidents and events but has its roots and sequences in an Eternal Order?

[13] Luke 6:21, 25.

CHAPTER XII

The Problem of Providence I

Difficulties in the Way of Belief in Providence offset by Difficulties in disbelieving it—The Idea of an Overruling Providence harmonizing Divine Direction and Human Freedom—Individual Providence, as distinguished from "Special Providences," testified to by a Host of Witnesses—The apparent Worthlessness of a vast Throng of Humans does not mean that they will always remain worthless—Divine Providence as related to Individual Freedom, and the resulting Complexity; the Effort toward a better Understanding of the Divine Will.

I

THE thought of Providence is coming to seem somewhat strange and old-fashioned to the typical modern man. It is associated in his mind with a narrow doctrinal outlook and a formal type of personal piety, impressive, often lovely, but belonging to the past. And yet the modern man, in spite of preoccupation with the physical and the procurable, is not without an undefined sense, at times, of something not unlike a Guiding Hand on the helm of the Ship of Souls which is bearing us all on into the Unknown. He would like to cherish a definite belief in Providence if it could be made reasonable to him. But such a faith, to be retained, he feels—not unrightly—must be modified and reconstructed to conform to the larger knowledge of the world in which we find ourselves.

The obstacles to belief in Providence, it must be admitted, are such as to create dismay. "A theism which seeks to establish such a solicitude for human welfare as has been attributed to the Christian God has an extremely difficult task," remarks a modern theologian.[1] Yet, on the other hand, *there are obstacles to disbelief in Providence also.* We find ourselves, in fact, between two opposing lines of inference. Some of our experiences seem to point to Providence, others, to refute it. What shall we conclude?

II

One of the chief obstacles to belief in Providence lies in the difficulty of harmonizing Divine Direction with the *freedom* which is so much a part of our everyday experience. Can both Guidance and freedom be true? If so, how can they be reconciled? This difficulty the older theology met by what was called an "Overruling Providence."

An Overruling Providence, as the phrase indicates, conceives of God as allowing men liberty to pursue their own ends, in their own ways, and then, without compro-

[1] Gerald B. Smith, "Is Theism Essential to Religion?" *The Journal of Religion,* July, 1925, p. 372.

mising freedom, reverses the effects of these blunders and misdeeds by swinging them into line with His all-wise and all-loving purpose in such a way as not only to straighten out the tangle but actually to bring good out of evil. Christian theology has not been alone in this conception. Stoicism, at its best, reflects something of the same idea. In the well-known *Hymn of Cleanthes* occur these words: "What is uneven Thy skill doth make even; what knew not order it setteth in order, and things that strive find all in Thee a friend. For thus hast Thou filled all, evil with good, in one great whole, so that in all things reigns one reason everlastingly." [2]

Whether or not human life as a whole can be construed in this light, certain events seem singularly to support it. A conspicuous instance (an old and favorite one) is the captivity of the Hebrew people. This catastrophe seemed to the captives utterly destructive of all their hopes and ideals; yet out of it came Israel's greatest gift to the world, *the conviction that God is the God of all peoples.*[3] Many historic wrongs, defeats, and disasters have issued in strange and unexpected good. The abuses of the Roman Catholic Church led to the Reformation. Dante's exile was prelude to the *Divine Comedy,* Milton's blindness to *Paradise Lost.* The tyranny of King John led to Magna Charta. In America the folly of George III led to the Declaration of Independence and the Consti-

---

[2] Davidson, *The Stoic Creed,* p. 235.

[3] "The Exile freed Jahweh as much as it enslaved the people; he became a God without bounds and therefore without bonds." E. W. Washburn, *The Origin and Evolution of Religion,* p. 282.

tution of the United States. Out of the stubborn iniquity
of slave-holding came the Declaration of Emancipation.
Out of the agony and wrong of the Great War have come
the League of Nations and the Treaty of Locarno. Of
course, one could point to any number of instances in
which no sign of good can be seen emerging from evil;
but who can be sure that in the end it may not prove
otherwise? The whole course of history receives light
from that most signal instance of an Overruling Providence, the crucifixion of Jesus. By virtue of some higher
law, or will, or wisdom, this act of deliberate injustice
and cruelty became the means by which a profound consciousness of the redeeming power of Love and the hope
of a transformed humanity entered the world. The dramatic and transforming result of this dark deed has made
the cross the center of human history. The symbol of
shame and defeat became the symbol of moral victory
and invincible love.

III

Yet a general Overruling Providence is not enough.
Can there be a Divinity that also shapes each one's ends,
rough-hew them how he will? Not of a kind, certainly,
that a petty and inconsequential type of Christian piety
has cherished. The common notion of a "Peddling Providence," as Goethe called it, is enough to discredit the very
idea of Providence. "Special providences" for oneself
and his relatives, general misfortunes for the rest of

mankind—such is the notion that has long cheapened the thought of Providence. This silly idea was sagaciously met by Archbishop Temple, according to a story told of him, in replying to a certain woman who came to him with the question: "Your Grace, my aunt was going to take the ten o'clock train last Friday and something occurred to prevent it, and the train was wrecked and every one on board killed or injured. Was not that a special Providence?" "Well, madam," answered the Archbishop, "not knowing your aunt I really cannot say."

From this childish notion of Providence it is a pleasure to turn to a more reasonable idea of individual Providence, such as that of which Plato wrote:

> We are then to think in this manner of the just man, that if he happens to be in poverty, or in diseases, or in any other of these imaginary evils, these things to him issue in something good, either whilst alive, or dead. For never at all is he neglected by the Gods at least, whoever he is who inclines earnestly to endeavor to become just, and practises virtue as far as it is possible for men to resemble God.[4]

This is not unlike the saying of Confucius: "There is Heaven—It knows me." Have such seers been mistaken? Or is there "a love that wills for each man a true, independent life"? [5]

Literature is full of such a belief in many forms. Confucius voiced it in the *Analects,* Laotze in the *Tao Teh King,* Plato in the *Apology,* Virgil in the *Aeneid,* Marcus

[4] *The Republic,* Book Ten [Spen's translation].
[5] Wilhelm Hermann, *Dogmatics.* Quoted by John R. Van Pelt, *The Methodist Review,* November, 1925.

Aurelius in his *Thoughts,* Epictetus in his *Discourses,* Dante in the *Divine Comedy,* Spenser in *The Faerie Queene,* Milton in *Samson Agonistes,* Pascal in the *Pensées,* Shakespeare in *The Tempest,* Wordsworth in *The Prelude,* Tennyson in the *Idylls of the King,* Lincoln in the *Second Inaugural Address,* Emerson in *Compensation,* Hugh Miller in *My Schools and Schoolmasters,* Tolstoi in *My Confession,* John Wesley in his *Journal,* Newman in his *Apologia,* Scott in *The Antiquary,* Kingsley in *Westward Ho,* Browning in *Ferishtah's Fancies,* Dickens in *Bleak House* and *Great Expectations,* Bryant in *To a Waterfowl,* Sidney Lanier in *The Marshes of Glynn,* Whittier in *My Psalm,* Holmes in *O Love Divine that Stooped to Share,* Longfellow in *Evangeline,* Helen Keller in *The Story of My Life* and *Out of the Dark,* Francis Thompson in *The Hound of Heaven,* John Muir in his *Letters,* George A. Gordon in *My Education and Religion.* Thousands of others have witnessed to an equally firm faith in Providence. Tens of thousands have felt what they could not express.

This is not so much a faith that God directly orders individual circumstances and events as that He is *with* the soul in all circumstances and events and thus gives to events their meaning and bearing. Paul spoke the revealing word when he said: "All things work together for good to them that love God." It is the insight of love alone that finds God in every experience. When one has that he sees in the compensations that follow loss, in the exchange of spiritual for temporal good, in the discipline that comes with disappointment and defeat, and in the "uses of adversity," a spiritual (rather than a temporal) Providence, and wins an ever deepening consciousness that he is "never at all neglected by God." This is "the Sovereign Goodness which governeth all things strongly and disposeth them sweetly," of which Boethius wrote from his prison chamber.[6] It takes both storm and sunshine to validate Providence.

> "I and my ancient self
> Long paths I've trod,
> The living light before,
> Behind, the rod:
> And in the beam and blow
> The misty God." [7]

H. G. Wells in *God the Invisible King,* after dismissing the idea of Providence, continues: "Cherish no delusions for yourself and others, you challenge danger and chance on your own strength; no talisman, no God, can help you or those you care for. Nothing of such things will God do; it is an idle dream. But God will be with you nevertheless. In the reeling aeroplane or the dark ice-cave God will be your courage. Though you suffer or are killed, it is not an end. He will be with you as you face death; he will die with you as he has died already countless myriads of brave deaths." But is not the Presence of God itself a Providence?

[6] *De Consolatione Philosophiæ.*
[7] Richard Wightman.

It is the universality of Providence that gives meaning to its individuality, and its individual character in turn interprets its universality. The Scotch saying, "Ilka blade o' grass has its drap o' dew," gains its fullest meaning when supplemented with what one may find suggested in the charming lines of Keats:

> "And every blade and every flower
> Pearlèd with the selfsame shower."

IV

It is not so difficult to conceive of God as guiding elect and sensitive spirits, but what of the vast throng of those apparently forgotten souls whom we call "the masses"? When one thinks of the hordes of his fellow beings, of the host of seemingly hopeless morons and defectives of all kinds, how is it possible to think of a Providence as over each of these?

The mind staggers at the thought of the vastness of the human race, as it does at the number of the stars, and still more at the apparent worthlessness of the great majority of men. The only way to find relief is to enlarge one's thought of God and His Fatherhood and to think of "the masses" not merely in terms of mass psychology but in the light of the possibilities of each human self. Who can say that death puts an end to these possibilities and does not rather open a new opportunity for their realization?

V

God with us in all the exigencies of life—so much of Providence, at least, is credible. Even H. G. Wells grants this, although he refuses to call it Providence. But must we stop here? Has not the Universal Presence something to do with *events* as well as being with us *in* them? Not that He completely *determines* events; for that is contradicted by everything without and within. Consciousness joins with observation in testifying that each of us acts freely, thereby adding either to the order or disorder of existing things. Whether we are metaphysically free or not, practically we are free, in sufficient measure, at least, to make a vast difference to ourselves and to our world. That we know.

Consider for a moment the immense consequences of every human being having a part in the intricate interplay of actions and events, starting consequences which go out in every direction in the lives of his fellows! The context of the everyday world thus becomes an apparently hopeless tangle, human and subhuman intelligences acting and reacting on each other, and, on the whole, in an amazing complex of relationships and consequences. In such a world it is rank unreason to lay upon God all the ill deeds and misfortunes that occur. "There is an ever recurring tendency in human nature," writes an acute observer, "which is aptly illustrated in the reply given the other day by a young acquaintance of my own who had been overtaken in a fault. 'No,' he asserted stoutly, when questioned concerning his personal responsibility in the matter, 'I don't blame it on myself. I blame it onto God.' " [8] And yet *above* all this confusion of interacting wills, and through it all, one can half detect, at times, the influence of a wise supremacy that keeps the whole complex fabric from incoherence and destruction. Conjunct with the multiplicity of disparate activities there are not wanting indications of the activity of One who at once grants liberty and limits it, keeps the ship of souls from mutiny and guides it toward a haven, however distant and unknown. In other words, there may be such a thing as Providence guiding events without ordering them.

No mechanistic or common-sense view of life can do away with the sense of a Divine Providence. The presence of a "misty God" in some way pervades life. The "laws of nature," as we call them, uniformities which run throughout the cosmos, while they constitute the observed and experienced order, do not suffice to explain it, but rather point toward Some One Beyond who is more than they, above them, through them, in them, making them serve a larger end. "Are they not all ministering servants sent forth to do service?"

Yet can we get a little nearer to deciphering the relation of Providence to particular events, or series of events, to our lives than this? Some happenings are manifestly the result of *our own acts,* intertwined with the acts of

[8] *The Atlantic Monthly,* Vol. 98, p. 533.

countless other human and subhuman agents and within the framework of certain uniformities that further or thwart them, but nevertheless in large measure due to our own action. Other happenings seem to come upon us without any responsibility of our own. Clearly the great boon, or the sad misfortune, which befell you yesterday was due to a complex of conspiring acts and counteracts—wills and forces—in which your own had little discernible part. Yet above and within this complexity there is room for a single intelligent presiding Will, keeping the whole interaction from being chaotic and meaningless, respecting the freedom of each, yet holding it within a larger good, and not unmindful of each separate self.

A more detailed study of the activity of the Supreme Will requires another chapter. Meanwhile let the whole subject be made more concrete and human by interjecting a moving passage from Hawthorne's *The House of Seven Gables,* in which the spent and distressed Hepzibah strives to send a prayer to Heaven:

Her faith was too weak, the prayer too heavy to be thus uplifted. It fell back a lump of lead upon her heart. It smote her with the wretched conviction, that Providence intermeddled not in these petty wrongs of one individual to his fellow, nor had any balm for these little agonies of a solitary soul; but shed its justice and its mercy, in a broad, sunlike sweep, over half the universe at once. Its vastness made it nothing. But Hepzibah did not see that, just as there comes a warm sunbeam into every cottage window, so comes a love-beam of God's care and pity, for every separate need.

CHAPTER XIII

The Problem of Providence II

The Recognition in the Lord's Prayer of the twofold Will of God,
Cosmic and Individual—The Prayer expresses Outreach after a larger
Good, individual and social—Divine Guidance an intelligent Conviction
on the Part of many, from Isaiah and Socrates to Tagore and John
Muir—Human Disasters not "Acts of God"; the Possibilities of the
Future—Earthquakes not necessarily Contradictions of Providence or
wholly without good Results—Life not a Playground but a School, in
which all Things work *together* for Good.

I

THERE is something profoundly significant in the
act of a devout mind when it makes its own that
majestic though self-abnegating affirmation of the Lord's
Prayer: "Thy will be done." This means more than
appears on the surface. Here is one of the paradoxes of
spiritual experience; for it involves a distinction, if one
may so describe it, between (1) the *cosmic* will of God
and (2) His *personal* will; a will that undergirds the
universe with uniformities which are for the general good,
and a will that concerns itself with the individual. Not,

180

of course, that these are two wills, but two aspects of the same Will.

This twofold relation of the will of God—to the whole and to the individual, to all and to each—naturally causes bewilderment and misunderstanding. The prayer "Thy will be done" rises above this misunderstanding. It recognizes that the individual is involved in a net of relations and consequences which is neither his creation nor his fault and which does not express the Divine Will toward him as an individual, but only as a member of the whole. Thus when the Christian prays, "Thy will be done tho' it be my own undoing," he accepts the cosmic will of God, even when it means disaster to himself, as best for him as a single individual involved in a great interrelated whole. At the same time he can see that the event might be entirely different were it the expression of the will of God to him as a separate, unrelated person. The misfortune which has befallen him may be, so to speak, the Father's *will* but not His *wish*. Thus when one prays, "Thy will be done," after some great personal loss or misfortune, he bends his will to the cosmic and general Will of God—recognizing it as best— even perceiving that it may work him good spiritually at the same time that it works him ill temporally.

Because of the total configuration of the universe, so to speak, the Divine Mind apparently obligates Himself to certain uniform methods of action which involve consequences to individuals that He may not desire but is unable, owing to the nature of the physical and moral orders, to prevent. Abraham Lincoln (as some one has pointed out) willed to push the war against the South through to a certain and speedy conclusion. In order to that end he willed, as incidental to it, all the loss and suffering necessary to secure it. But he did not do so "willingly." He would have prevented the bloodshed and sorrow at any cost to himself, if he could have done so.

In the mighty complex of His universe, produced by wills and ways innumerable, from the activity of electrons and amebæ to the wilful waywardness of men, the Supreme Person, in guiding it all to the best issue, may not be able (speaking reverently) to accomplish for the individual at any given moment just what He desires for him in exemption from the consequences of the acts of others or in the operation of natural laws. In praying, "Thy will be done," the reverent soul recognizes this, adapts himself to it, and seeks to find, even in adversity, a still deeper will of God. In that moving cry of an afflicted soul, the third chapter of *Lamentations*, with its alternating grief and hope, protest and submission, may be found an anticipation of this affirmation of the Lord's Prayer. This is no supernormal pietism, but "proving what is that good and acceptable and perfect will of God which is our reasonable service." It grounds in the faith that God works for the good of each in the good of all and for the good of all in that of each.

II

Yet the petition is larger than this, too. It is one not of submission only but of outreach. One who offers it may make it a prayer for the fulfillment of the will of God, in the sense of the Divine *purpose,* not for himself only but for others. The will of God for all—the fulfillment of His purpose for neighbor, kinsman, nation, church, race—all this comes within the compass of this brief petition, as the sun is reflected in a drop of dew.

The comprehensiveness and true piety of the simple affirmation, "Thy will be done," are beyond expression. In it are at once submission, and desire, consent and petition. It is a confession that whatever is is right as regards the Divine part in it, but in need of righting as regards the human part. It is at once an approval of the cosmic order, a prayer for the redemption of the social order, and a petition for the right attitude as respects oneself. In view of human solidarity it is a sorrowful recognition that oneself and his fellows are not living according to the Divine will and a deep and heartfelt desire that we may come to do so.

In one of his moods of ardent reflection, St. Augustine, musing upon the imperfections of this lower world in which "all these things which are not suitable to one another are yet suitable to that lower half of creation called earth, which has its own windy and cloudy sky of like nature with itself," finds satisfaction in this thought:

"But, seeing that in heaven all Thy angels praise Thee, Praise Thee, O God, in the height, and all Thy hosts, sun and moon, all stars of light, the heaven of heavens and the waters that be above the heavens praise Thy name (Ps. 148), seeing this, I say, I no longer desired a better world, because my thought ranged over all, and with a sounder judgment I reckoned that things above were better than things below, *yet that all creation together was better than the things above.*" [1] "All creation together . . . better than the things above"? Yes, providing the things above are coming down into the things below, as the Seer of Patmos saw, and the things below are moving upward into the things above, so that more and more the two realms are becoming one. In such a universe the prayer, "Thy will be done on earth, as it is in Heaven," becomes the deft touch which opens the door between the "But" and the "Ben" of the Father's House.

III

Yet something besides the sense of Presence and the movement of the Divine Will above and within the flow of events is, as we have already indicated. enwrapped within the meaning of what is termed Providence. It is what is perhaps best termed *Guidance*—the subtle impulsion, as of a Gracious Hand, toward one's task in life, or some great good, or toward a comrade spirit or one

[1] *Confessions*, Book VI, Chapter 13 (Italics are mine).

whom he can help or be helped by.   Many responsive spirits have felt such an impulsion.

It comes to men in various ways—in the intensely real impression of it which often seizes upon one who is called to a responsible position, or one who is moved to creative work in literature, music or art; or in the constraint which sends one on some hard duty or adventure —such as Isaiah felt when he responded to the voice in the temple saying: Who will go for us? "Here am I, send me," or such as Paul felt when he wrote, "The love of Christ constraineth me"; or such as the Maid of Orleans felt when she girded on her armor and went out to lead the army of France to victory; or such as moved St. Francis when he wedded Lady Poverty; or such as Tagore felt when he wrote, "This little flute of a reed thou hast carried over hills and dales, and hast breathed through it melodies ever new"; or such as John Muir experienced when he said, "I feel as if a Divine Hand had been laid on my shoulder"; or—to go back to an early and memorable example—such as Socrates felt when his guiding spirit (*dæmon*) bade him face his accusers in undisturbed confidence of rectitude.

It is true that a superficial psychology has a very plausible and omniscient way of disposing of such experiences as mere subjective reactions to *stimuli*, internal or external, or both; but this account, while it may help to understand these experiences on the side of their psychophysical nature, does not explain them, any more than "capillary attraction" explains why a tree grows, or evolution explains why the universe has come to be what it is.

Future generations will look back upon ours with astonishment that we should have been so ready, even avid, to take explanations of function and method for ultimate explanations. It is not necessary to credit every hectic claim of a peculiar vision or a special mission as a revelation of Divine Guidance. There are bound to be many "false prophets" for every true one, many visionaries who "follow wandering fires, lost in the quagmire" for one who sees the Holy Grail. Yet the sane, strong, steady souls who humbly believe that they have Divine commissions, and go far to prove it by what they do, are not to be discredited because of the many who take their own fancies for Divine communications. "By their works ye shall know them." The valiant soul who says to himself: "This humble task, which is not of my choosing, is given me to do and in doing it I am fulfilling a Will wiser and better than my own," gives as fine evidence of sagacity, as well as sincerity, as life affords.

IV

And yet, if a Divine Providence is over men manifesting itself in the sense of Presence and the guidance of the Spirit, why should the exigencies of life be so great and so constant? What a blind succession of ills life seems often to be, shocking one with every newspaper he takes up and leaving him with the sense of living in a world not only "out of joint" but never yet jointed and incapable of becoming so! The large number of these disasters arising from carelessness, or recklessness, and therefore preventable, does not cause so much perplexity. But what of those that are due to what the insurance companies, with remarkable religiousness, call "acts of God"? Are they "acts of God" or only acts of His world—a world in which every accident is according to law (for the most part ascertainable law) and thus the scene of a Providence whose concern, perhaps, is not so much to prevent accidents as to have men learn to avoid them.

In attempting to form some understanding of the total "configuration"—to use again the term of the *Gestalt* psychology—in which we find ourselves, it is necessary to take into consideration vast areas of *space-time,* backward and forward. This may be disheartening, or enheartening, as one looks at it. To our generation, as to none before, has come the revelation of the enormous period that has been required to make our world what it is, and ourselves what we are. This is by no means a disheartening disclosure. In the light of it what transformations may not occur in the future, not only to the race as a whole but to each individual member of it! In a reverie, entitled *In the Fens,* Arthur C. Benson writes thus:

I came to-day to a dyke which had been recently heightened, to guard against the winter floods. They had dug out the blue galt for the purpose, and I could see the pale line of it run for miles over the level. I picked up one of the spadefuls idly; it was dried and laminated like slate; I broke it across, and there in the clay lay a sprinkling of tiny fossils,—small water-shells crushed flat, creatures that looked like great woodlice, with armored carapaces, things like stalks of water-weed. Wherever I broke the block it was the same. How many thousand years ago, I wondered, had these shells and insects lived out their lives in the great lagoon! They had lived and died; they had sunk to the bottom of the lake; the ooze had covered them year by year. Every spadeful of the clay along the dyke-bank was full of the same creatures, each a monument of a tiny individual life. What an inscrutable and illimitable prospect it opened to the mind! What was the purpose, the meaning of it all? Each of these tiny creatures had had his taste of life; they had been all in all to them-selves, even as I am to-day to myself, conscious of their own minute existence, and perhaps dimly aware of a vast world of shadowy existences outside of them. They had loved life; they had hated death and darkness. And yet, with all our inventiveness and sagacity and complacent wisdom, we are no nearer to knowing the why and wherefore of it all,—what it is that thrusts us into being, and why that being is withdrawn.

Somehow, in the thought of this immensity of life, unrolling itself so patiently through the ages, I felt a strange sense of unreality about my own little hopes and fears, so terribly urgent and significant to me, so hopelessly minute in the eye of the Father of all living. One can learn more from that little cube of clay than from all the sermons of the divines. Not a hopeful lesson, perhaps, not stimulating, or what is called inspiring; but the truth of it, which at first sight seems ghastly and insupportable, brings in its wake a thought of intense significance; it hints at an enormous patience, an un-ceasing energy; it makes the dreams of man pale and unsub-stantial; it assures one that, strive and fret as one may, there is something to be apprehended which man cannot teach; it brings with it an intense resignation, a tranquil determination to wait and see what God is doing for us.[2]

"To wait and see what God is doing for us"—that is true wisdom.

V

Among the natural disasters that create a doubt of Providence, none is greater and more disturbing than an earthquake. Having experienced one of the worst of these in America in recent times (San Francisco, 1906) and having closely observed the immediate results of another (Santa Barbara, 1925), perhaps I may venture to give the impressions of a near-at-hand observer. The first thing that has struck me about an earthquake is, of course, the earthquake itself and the next is that it seldom occurs wholly without previous warning. Those who live in an earthquake belt know that one may take place at any moment. They know, therefore, that they should build—as they are just beginning to do—accordingly. Earthquakes do not happen causelessly or maliciously. Modern science understands their cause and how to prepare for them.

The second reflection that comes to one is that an earthquake, occurring, as it does, in the process of earth-making, goes with the kind of beings we are and the kind of globe we inhabit. We ourselves are unfinished; our world is unfinished. The correspondence may be more significant than we realize. It doubtless would seem

[2] *Atlantic Monthly,* vol. 98, p. 833.

preferable to live on a finished earth, one that has passed beyond all youthful caprices, but perhaps if it were firmer it might be colder. At any rate, although our planet has not yet become mature, it is "a goodly frame." Its growing tremors play havoc, as in a judgment day, with all defective and faulty construction, but that which is sound and well constructed, as a rule, stands. At least, it is so in California.

The third fact about an earthquake that has impressed me is that, despite its toll of loss and suffering, it shakes men into much more sensitive and sympathetic relations with each other. They suddenly become more human. Those of us who passed through the San Francisco earthquake can never forget the wave of brotherliness that swept over the Bay region following the first fright and grief. For a little while, at least, men rose to heights of courage and helpfulness such as made life seem a great spiritual association in goodwill.

It would be childish to say these considerations make earthquakes understandable and desirable events in the general scheme of things. Yet such by-products of disaster cannot be left out of account and may well lead one to hesitate to demand that this be a quakeless world in order to be a good one.

VI

It is hopeless to try to solve the problem of Providence if one approaches it from the viewpoint of a world made for human security, pleasure, and ease. Viewed as a recreation center, life offers a sorry and distressing spectacle. Viewed as a school—with a playground attached—the products of which are discipline, character, personality, it presents quite another aspect.

Nor is it possible to regard the world as a providential order if one views it from a static, individualistic, and localized standpoint. Things do not work for good separately, as the apostle saw, but *together*. Although we cannot take in the whole of things and events, we can at least conceive of a Mind capable of viewing the whole. This gives tone to one's whole attitude toward life and the universe. It enables him to believe in an *invisible* Providence working toward ends yet indiscernible and far ahead. "Of this universal providence," wrote Swedenborg, "man sees nothing. If he did see it, it would seem only as one passing sees heaps and accumulated material from which a house is to be built, while the Lord sees it as a magnificent palace, with the work of construction and enlargement constantly going on." [3] These are wise words. Yet to say that one sees *nothing* of the universal providence is hardly just. Little as one can see of the Divine Purpose, it is enough to enable him to say, with Dante:

"In la sua volontade e' nostra pace." [4]

[3] *Divine Providence,* § 203.
[4] "In His will is our peace."

PART IV

Effects

CHAPTER XIV

Life in the Light of Divine Fatherhood

The first beneficent Effect of Belief in God as Father upon Life to be noted is that it makes One feel at Home in the Universe—A second Effect is to promote the Spirit of Gratitude, as it finds expression, *e.g.,* in the old and beautiful Custom of Grace before Meat—A third Effect is to encourage Prayer, which opens receptive Channels and puts One into right Relations with his Fellows and with God—A fourth Effect is to sustain the Moral Order, especially as relates to the Family, whose Integrity is now seriously threatened.

NO DISCUSSION of the Fatherhood of God would be complete which failed to take account of the practical effects of such a faith. That these effects are very real, there can be no reasonable doubt. A genuine and sustained belief in God as our spiritual Father is capable of transforming life and making all things new. As Epictetus wrote: "If a person could be persuaded of this principle as he ought, that we are all originally descended from God, and that he is the father of men and gods; I conceive he would never think of himself meanly or ignobly." What such a faith can accomplish has been demonstrated by millions of loyal lives lived in its light. Even so depreciative a critic of mystical religion as Professor Leuba grants that "to live, and to be loved by, a good and all-powerful Person is the most effective way to vivify the human heart and to fulfill its essential yearnings." [1]

I

One of the most beneficent results of such a faith is *to make one feel more at home in the universe.* Science cannot do this for us, in spite of its banishment of the demons of superstition and ignorance and the securities with which it has encompassed us. Science can write a *Materia Medica,* but only religion can produce the twenty-third psalm. As a scientifically integrated succession of events and experiences, life may become comparatively safe, comfortable, agreeable, but hardly happy and hopeful. That requires something more. Religion, alone, can make the universe homelike, giving one—in place of what has been called "astronomical intimidation"—a sense of the friendliness of the stars, the mystic meaning of the sunshine, and the ultimate beneficence of the storm, affording deliverance from the snare of that fierce fowler the microbe and from the noisome pestilences that attend "advanced civilization," by implanting an assurance that none of these can injure the soul that is in the care of God; above all imparting that sense of Presence which is the joy of those who dwell deep.

Of this sense of the Divine Presence in nature few more

[1] *The Psychology of Religious Mysticism,* p. 280.

stirring expressions can be found than a passage from Walter Pater's *Marius the Epicurean,* which is so beautiful and full of meaning that I cannot refrain quoting from it at length:

. . . He [Marius] sat down in an olive-garden, and, all around him and within still turning to reverie, the course of his own life hitherto seemed to withdraw itself into some other world, disparted from this spectacular point where he was now placed to survey it, like that distant road below, along which he had travelled this morning across the Campagna. Through a dreamy land he could see himself moving, as if in another life, and like another person, through all his fortunes and misfortunes, passing from point to point, weeping, delighted, escaping from various dangers. That prospect brought him, first of all, an impulse of lively gratitude: it was as if he must look round for some one else to share his joy with; for some one to whom he might tell the thing, for his own relief. Companionship, indeed, familiarity with others, gifted in this way or that, or at least pleasant to him, had been, through one or another long span of it, the chief delight of the journey. And was it only the resultant general sense of such familiarity, diffused through his memory, that in a while suggested the question whether there had not been—besides Flavian, besides Cornelius even, and amid the solitude which in spite of ardent friendship he had perhaps loved best of all things—some other companion, an unfailing companion, ever at his side throughout; doubling his pleasure in the roses by the way, patient of his peevishness or depression, sympathetic above all with his grateful recognition, onward from his earliest days, of the fact that he was there at all? Must not the whole world around have faded away for him altogether, had he been left for one moment really alone in it? In his deepest apparent solitude there had been rich entertainment. It was as if there were not one only, but two wayfarers, side by side, visible there across the plain, as he indulged his fancy. A bird came and sang among the wattled hedge-roses: an animal feeding crept nearer: the child who kept it was gazing quietly: and the scene and the hours still conspiring, he passed from that mere fantasy of a self not himself, beside him in his coming and going, to those divinations of a living and companionable spirit at work in all things, of which he had become aware from time to time in his old philosophic readings—in Plato and others, last but not least, in Aurelius. Through one reflection upon another, he passed from such instinctive divinations, to the thoughts which give them logical consistency, formulating at last, as the necessary exponent of our own and the world's life, that reasonable Ideal to which the Old Testament gives the name of *Creator*, which for the philosophers of Greece is the *Eternal Reason*, and in the New Testament the *Father of Men*—even as one builds up from act and word and expression of the friend actually visible at one's side, an ideal of the spirit within him.

This is Pater's Christian mysticism read into a young Roman's mind, but it puts into language something which devout minds in many generations have deeply, even though indistinctly, felt. To experience in the gladness of morning something of the joy of the creative love of God, at noontide the refreshment of His all-sustaining strength, and in the hush of evening something of a "peace that passeth all understanding"—this is to find the world a temple filled with "divinations of a living and companionable spirit at work in all things."

It would be unjust to assume that nothing of this kind was experienced before Christianity came to intensify it.

It finds tender and vivid expression in the twenty-third and ninety-first psalms. The religious literature of India is replete with it—voiced anew, in relation to the Living Christ, by Mahatma Gandhi, in the following interview:

The question was asked of Mr. Gandhi: "How do you feel, not only about the Christ of history, the Christ of Judea, but about the living Christ, the Christ of the Resurrection?"

Mr. Gandhi replied: "If I understand correctly my friend's very sincere question, he wants to know whether I feel within me the presence of the living Christ. If the living Christ is the same as the historical Christ, then I must confess that I do not feel that presence. If 'Christ' is a controvertible term with 'God,' the living God, not a God who lives somewhere in the Himalayas or in the clouds, but God who lives nearer to me than any one of you, nearer to me than my hands and feet, if that is your meaning of Christ, then I say that both Krishna and Christ live in me, because to me they are controvertible terms. I do not talk now of the historical Krishna, but I talk of the seer, the one who is supposed to have given the Gita. And yet I do not even mean the one who is supposed to have given the Gita. What I mean is something which is indefinable, which is inexpressible. If, then, you will allow me to interpret the living Christ as that indefinable Essence, I believe in that Christ. If I did not realize the presence of that living, speaking God in me, I should become a raving maniac. . . . Only the Presence, the realization of the Presence, enables me to keep body and soul together, and, in spite of all that disturbs me from outside, I enjoy in an abundant measure an inexpressible peace." [2]

Yet it is not the mystic alone who has this sense of a Divine Companion. The simple faith that this is God's

[2] *The Missionary Review of the World,* December, 1925.

world, and He its Father and ours, sweetens and strength-
ens the lives of thousands who are not conscious mystics,
yet who dwell in the secret place of the Most High and
abide under the shadow of the Almighty.

II

Faith in God as Father fosters not only trust, but
gratitude. The cultivation of this fitting and beautiful
form of piety has long been associated with the life of
the family, especially in the use of "grace before meat."
Is this custom about to become obsolete? It must be
confessed that there is much in modern life to rob this
honored family practice of its meaning and naturalness.
One can appreciate something of the simple piety and fitness of the act when the Roman *pater familias,* in the
days before the great corruption, took the handful of
meal from the table and threw it upon the fire as a thank
offering, or when "in some cottage far apart" of old
Scotia, as described by Burns, "the priest-like father"
lifted his voice in humble thanksgiving. It is not difficult
to think that God "may hear well-pleased the language of
the soul" that rises thus. But, "times have changed."
Can grace at table mean anything real to a modern
family, aware that the profits of their breakfast foods
build sumptuous palaces at Pasadena and Miami, that
their meats come out of the stockyards of Chicago, that
between their bread and pastry and the wheat fields of
the Northwest lie the woes of the unfortunate farmer

and the conscienceless cornerings of Wall Street; and that even their fruits and vegetables are tainted by the profits of middlemen and the toil of despised and sometimes insulted aliens?

These changed conditions cannot but color, even if they do not take all character and meaning from, grace at table. Yet they do not essentially change the almost mystically revivifying quality of food nor destroy the fitness and joyousness of a thankful heart. All the iniquities of monopolies and combinations, the contentions of capital and labor, the congested profits of middlemen, and the economic waste that intervene between the soil and the consumer together cannot alter the fact that wholesome foods come from the bountiful earth, nourished by sun and rain and that they delight the taste as well as nourish and sustain life. Money buys them but money does not produce them, nor does mere labor. The gift quality lingers about them and cannot be eradicated. The table talk of Luther still sounds wholesome and human as he exclaims upon the pity that men do not take the good things of life in simple enjoyment and gratitude.

Yet food and other enjoyments of the senses find a superphysical value in something which transcends and speaks through them.

"Sometimes there comes a taste surpassing sweet
Of common things,—the very breath I take;
A draught from some cool spring amid the brake;
The wheaten crust that I in hunger eat.

> So I have thought that Heaven, perhaps, is just
> The uttermost perception of all good,
> The spiritual rapture of this zest, refined;
> An exquisite new taste of friendship, food,
> The joys of love, the odors in the wind,
> And all that now seems deadened by our dust."[3]

Behind all that goes to make life glad and good, all forces, circumstances, influences, gifts, persons, that have conspired to make one's lot happy—there exists a Power, or Person, without whom none of these can be accounted for and toward whom the thankful heart finds its way through and beyond them all. At least that has been the experience of countless grateful souls.

But what of those who have little—pitifully little—of the gifts and opportunities of life? When one thinks of them is not his gratitude suddenly chilled?

> "Who has given me this sweet?
> And given my brother dust to eat
> And when will his ship come in?"

But it is not God who gives men dust to eat. His gifts are wholesome and pure. It is *we* who give our brothers dust to eat. And *Everyman's* ship will come in when we learn to share the good gifts of God.

III

With gratitude there goes, also, as its natural accompaniment—if there is a Fatherly God—*asking, outreach,*

[3] James Buckham, *The Heart of Life,* p. 48.

prayer. If there is an All-Giver, the natural sequence is, in the words of Jesus, "How much more shall he give good things *to them that ask him.*"

The sequences of the spiritual world are as orderly and reliable as those of the natural world. "The Father which seeth in secret shall reward thee openly." Is this any stranger, less believable, less natural, than the sequence of the invisible electron and the arc light, or that of the miniature seed and the giant sequoia? We are in the midst of a universe of marvelous potencies, natural and spiritual; it is folly to leave them unused, because their working is beyond our power to understand.

Prayer—the personal communion of the finite person with the Infinite Person—opens channels through which flow all manner of gifts, insights, conferrings of truth and grace, impartations of spiritual life and strength. It also opens the way to the hearts of others. To gain right relations with one's fellows—to break down barriers, to remove hostile and indifferent feelings, to weave threads of interest and affection about others which become firm as steel—one has but to unite himself with them, through the All-Father, by prayer. There is no magic in this, yet it acts like magic—the magic of the laws of the spiritual life.

It is a common mistake to conceive of prayer as a substitute for action. Prayer *is* action—"noble, sublime, godlike action." When one desires to *do* something for another, yet can find no *outer* deed to do, let him *pray.* For thus he enacts a deed which enters as a potent factor into the great invisible arena of spiritual action which constitutes the deepest reality of life.

The whole meaning and ministry of prayer—its philosophy, its ethic, its practice—lies within the compass of the truth of Divine Fatherhood. To practice prayer means to realize the true meaning of Divine Fatherhood. Those who, through any difficulty raised (or supposed to have been raised) by science, or philosophy, or common sense, have given up the practice of prayer as childish may well ask themselves if they have not, through a hasty and ill-judged inference, lost hold of one of the most natural, reasonable, and elevating activities of the human spirit.

IV

Not only does faith in Divine Fatherhood foster a harmonious attitude toward the universe and toward others but *it underlies and sustains the moral order to an extent which is seldom recognized.* It not only supplies the perfect ideal—"Be ye therefore perfect, even as your Father which is in heaven is perfect"—it also furnishes the basis and inspiration of a sane, practical, working ethic, firm enough to keep human life from disintegration. "Let a man say wholeheartedly 'Our Father who art in heaven' and other men come alive for him as they never will apart from the thought and the worship of God." [4] Probe any other philosophy of life than

[4] Willard L. Sperry, *Reality in Worship*, p. 345.

Christianity to its foundations and it proves insufficient to sustain the weight of a social structure which has reached the range and complexity of modern life.

That basal social unit, the family, grounds in Divine Fatherhood and gets its sacred character therefrom. Paul, with his deep discernment of underlying realities, perceived this when he wrote to the Christians of Ephesus—that affluent, Orientalized Græco-Roman city in which the cult of the Great Mother tended to disintegrate and dishonor family life: "For this reason, then, I kneel before the Father from whom every family in heaven and on earth derives its name and nature, praying Him out of the wealth of his glory to grant you a mighty increase of strength by his Spirit in the inner man." [5]

One of the exigencies for which moral and spiritual strength is most needed to-day is to keep the family life from going on the rocks. The present widespread disposition to depreciate the family tie, to regard it as a social construct which can be treated as convenience and pleasure dictate, is far more serious than is ordinarily realized. No doubt modifications of family life, to conform to changed social and economic conditions, are not only warranted but demanded; but to strike at the sacredness of the marriage tie, as grounded in reverence for personality and personal loyalty, means to sever the root of the tree of home life and cause to wither leaf, blossom, and fruit. Human life thrives best and yields its best

[5] Eph. 3:14-16 (Moffatt). This translation brings out the full meaning of the original by the use of the words "name and nature."

fruits—individual and social, marital and communal—when grounded in faith in an eternal, constitutive Perfect Personality, Author and Guardian of the moral order—to sin against whom is to darken one's own life and that of others.

The Brotherhood of Man—upon what does *it* rest, unless upon the Fatherhood of God? Our descent from a common simian ancestry carries with it only physical kinship, not the kind of fraternity that makes one *brotherly,* to say nothing of "laying down his life for his friends." That the same blood flows in all our veins means much, but it is far from sufficient to make men real brothers. Sonship of a common Spiritual Father alone constitutes a true brotherhood—one that reaches down into the depths of human nature and leads to far-reaching, practical results. The consideration of what such a brotherhood means calls for a separate chapter.

CHAPTER XV

Human Brotherhood

Human Converse environed and deepened by the Sense of Presence—
Discontent with wrong Human Relations aroused by the Consciousness
of Divine Fatherhood, in spite of the apparent Indifference of Christians to Economic and Social Inequalities—Christians as Rectifiers of
Social and Individual Wrongs—Two Ideals of realized Human Good,
One temporal, the Other Eternal—Christianity's Endeavor to harmonize
these as embodied in Christ's Ideal of the Kingdom of God, with its
twofold Aspect—This Kingdom, founded on Divine Fatherhood and
Human Brotherhood, is by its very Nature, both temporal and eternal,
personal and social, present and coming.

I

THE fatherhood of God and the brotherhood of man
are closely associated in the Christian philosophy
of life. Is this a mere formal convention or is it grounded
in something elemental and essential? One of the most
clear-visioned Christian writers has said: "Christianity
holds that the incentive and the will to practise the
brotherhood of man depend upon the constant adoration
of God as father. If men were to cease the worship of
God the greatest single incentive to fraternal ways among

men would be withdrawn." [1]   This is a strong statement, but not without foundation.   For the relations of men to one another, as far as they rise above mere external contacts, reveal an indefinable, mystical character which involves something more than mere human relationships. Human fellowship is enveloped in a sense of *Presence*— the psychologist would call it, perhaps, a coconsciousness. This is no imaginary thing, but a very real and persuasive influence.   We meet and hold converse with one another in this enveloping Presence, spiritually, as in the circumambient air physically, although we may not be vividly conscious of either of these environing realities except at times of peculiar sensitiveness.   "There is *Something* more important than you or me that brings us together," said a friend to me once on parting—and he a professor of philosophy.   "That which is capable of the innermost appropriation by the individual and at the same time is able to establish the deepest fellowship between individuals—that is the Holiest," writes Höffding.[2]   And that is the Personal God.

The consciousness of Presence sensitizes moral obligation.   The sense of sin and penitence which follows a wrong done to others is bound up with the conviction that the act is a wrong also to One in whom the Moral Law has its Source and Sanction.   The full meaning of moral offense is not, cannot be, realized until one comes to

---

[1] Willard Sperry, *op. cit.*, p. 165.
[2] H. Höffding, *Philosophy of Religion*, p. 375.

realize with the psalmist, "Against *Thee* have I sinne[d]
Nor will the full force of social injustice be felt, as
prophets of Israel felt it, until it is seen not only
against humanity but as against the Guardian of the
moral order.

II

Faith in God as Father has a twofold effect. While it
brings those who hold it into harmony with life, and with
the universe and other selves, at the same time it makes
them deeply dissatisfied with all that subverts and hinders
the Divine Will by oppression and wrong. It begets both
a quiet content and a noble discontent. It produces reliance upon the Divine purpose and processes and also
an impulse to work, as well as pray, for a new and better
world.

If one desires evidence of this twofold motivation, let
him turn to the prophets of Israel. The nearer they approached to the Universal Fatherhood of God, finding an
inner peace, the more were they consumed with social
passion for the righting of wrong and the establishment
of justice. The same is true in far greater degree of
Jesus, the steady ardor of whose confidence in God as
Father kindled the flame of his desire to establish a kingdom of righteousness and brotherhood. "Jesus was both
evolutionist and revolutionist," a believer in the law of
orderly development and in the active righting of wrong.

[3] Ps. 51:4—Moffatt's translation. "Thee only" is too restrictive to
represent the psalmist's feeling. "Thee chiefly" might come nearer to it.

He who said, "Not one jot or tittle of the law shall fail till all be fulfilled," cried, "Repent, for the Kingdom of God is at hand."

The passionate longing for a redeemed human life is wrought into the very substance of the Lord's prayer and into the very nature of Christianity. It is true that history, superficially read, appears to make Christianity the bulwark of conservatism. Have not the believers in the Fatherhood of God been the upholders of the established order, defenders of privileges and inequalities? Have not the true social reformers, the battlers for social justice, the champions of the submerged classes, been iconoclasts, freethinkers, infidels, men like Rousseau, Shelley, Tom Paine, James Mill, Karl Marx? Without disparaging the devotion and service of these men or of any—of whatsoever faith or unfaith—who have thrown themselves into the great task of social betterment, it is not the radicals who have done most for human uplift. The meteors catch the eye, but it is the planets and the fixed stars that light the sky of social progress.

III

Those who have done most for human advancement have been men with faith in God. It was Christianity as it spread its renewing, humanizing spirit through the arid wastes of a decadent civilization, breaking down social barriers, lifting the slave into fellowship with his master, introducing a new ethic of love and goodwill, that

sowed the seed of a new social order and impelled humanity forward. And this was largely because Jesus taught
men to believe that God is their Father and that as His
sons they should live as brothers. Recall such vital
groups in the history of social progress as the Benedictines, Franciscans, Brethren of the Common Life, Lol-
lards, Waldenses, Anabaptists, Wesleyans, the founders
of Social Settlements—were they not all inspired by a
great faith in human brotherhood and Divine Fatherhood,
gained from Christ?

Granted that "the red fool-fury of the Seine" was a
cleansing flood and prepared the way for true democracy;
it had no constructive power. Granted that the Reformation became in time the tool of nationalism and privilege,
nevertheless it was a great liberating force. The regeneration of Geneva was accomplished by a man, who, if he
did not grasp the true meaning of Divine Fatherhood,
did at least endeavor to make the Sovereign Righteous
Will supreme. Holland's republicanism was largely a
Christian product; so was Scotland's uprising under
Knox. Cromwell was in some of his ideas a narrow
fanatic, but it was his religious zeal that made him the
scourge of triviality and tyranny. That is a fine tribute
to Puritanism which Chesterton paid when he wrote:
"Nothing can efface the essential distinction that Puritanism was one of the world's great efforts after the discovery of the true order, whereas it was the essence of the
Restoration that it involved no effort at all."

The abolition of slavery—to whom was it due? To

men, in the main, like Wilberforce and Shaftesbury and other great Christians in England and to the antislavery agitators of New England—Samuel Hopkins, Garrison, Wendell Phillips, John Brown, Whittier, John Woolman, and their comrades—men steeped in the spirit of the Lord's Prayer and faith in a God who cares. Prison Reform, the Abolition of Child Labor, the Red Cross, Peace Societies, and a score of similar movements have been the work in the main of men and women of Christian faith and temper. To whom does the chief credit belong for that great social crusade in behalf of the people as a whole, the Prohibition Movement, slowly, persistently working its way forward—joined at length by economists and business men because they saw its economic value—if not to the "temperance fanatics" in the churches?

It has been men and women of Christian faith, chiefly, who have "done things" for humanity. It is true that toil and sacrifice for social upbuilding have been shared by many who have revolted from a merely formal and churchly Christianity yet have been on the side of the angels—unawares. Nor should one overlook the service of those who have been pure revolutionists, consumed with hatred for tyranny, and who saw no further than crushing out wrong. It is true also that class interest and demand for just treatment on the part of Labor have played, doubtless, the chief part in bringing about industrial improvement. But, silently and forcefully coöperating with every humanitarian advance, has been the sense of Divine law and Divine love which Christianity has instilled.

It is those who have been animated and upheld by the conviction, "If God be for us who can be against us?" who have spent themselves most freely for a better world and never despaired, who have launched *Mayflowers* on wintry seas, and written the literature of social regeneration —a *Utopia*, a *New Atlantis*, a *Sartor Resartus*, a *Fors Clavigera*,[4] a *Christianizing the Social Order*—who have founded hospitals and social settlements and organized and maintained societies for every sort of humanitarian object, who have investigated coal strikes and pushed forward the improvement of industrial conditions.

IV

Religion has cherished two contrasted social ideals, one on this earth, the other in a world above, or beyond, the present. The two most marked instances of this contrast are to be found in Israel and India—Israel, with her ideal of a Messianic Kingdom on earth, in which the dark side of life disappears in a redeemed social order enriched with all earthly blessings and all human relationships glorified; India, with her ideal of escape from the evils of life in Nirvana, a state of pure being, "not blown upon" in which sight, sense, and sound, and all physical

[4] "In speaking of Mr. Ruskin's moral standard of ideas, it is essential to recognize that his foundation is not ethics but theology; moral sentiments are not ultimate and self-existent things; but are effluences of divinity." J. A. Hobson, *John Ruskin, Social Reformer*, p. 43.

contacts and relationships, fade like a dream and are gone.

The first of these ideals tends to subordinate spiritual to physical well-being, and to merge the individual in social redemption; the second tends to depreciate the values of life here and now, to ignore social righteousness, to conceive of the goal as either absorption into, or full and undisturbed communion with, the Eternal.

Zoroastrianism and Mohammedanism furnish another striking contrast in this regard—the former throwing all its ardor into the winning of an earthly Utopia, the latter picturing a sensuous. individualistic immortality in a life beyond.

V

Christianity is unique in its attempt to embrace and harmonize both of these ideals. The Kingdom of God is at once a purified social order upon earth and an invisible spiritual Kingdom.

The difficulty of understanding this twofold ideal has lent perplexity to Jesus' conception of the Kingdom. At one time he seems to regard it as a redeemed social order, to be ushered in soon and by dramatic events; again he appears to be thinking of a purely spiritual Kingdom— "within" rather than without—consisting of fellowship with others and with God.

It has been insisted upon by opposing schools of New Testament scholars that we choose one of these ideals as Jesus' real conception and abandon the other. But this is to create a false issue. Jesus' idea of the Kingdom is left in confusion in the Gospels—owing, probably, largely to the failure of his disciples to comprehend his full meaning—but there are many indications that it was strikingly ethical, original, and comprehensive.[5]

The following outlines of his thought of the Kingdom may be detected through the haze of his reported sayings:

(1) The life of the Kingdom is ethical and spiritual. Its quality makes it eternal.[6] Not to have this kind of life is to be practically dead. The unawakened, Jesus seems to imply, have so little of real life that they are already more dead than living. "Follow me; and let the dead bury their dead," he said to one who would become his disciple. This sounds harsh and inhuman, little in keeping with Jesus' customary tenderness; but it is no more than urgent moral issues often require. The volunteer in any great cause must be ready, not to renounce, but to leave kinship ties and duties behind him for the sake of greater service. There is no other way.

(2) Whatever eschatological ideas gathered about the idea of the Kingdom in the mind of Jesus, the *time* and *manner* of its coming were subordinate to its *character*.[7]

---

[5] "If we conceive of Jesus merely as the herald of a future kingdom we take the keystone out of his teaching and out of the whole story of his life." E. F. Scott, *The Ethical Teaching of Jesus*, p. 44.

[6] "It was part of Jesus' religious experience to believe that such a life [*i.e.*, of likeness to God] possessed the eternal quality. It was good enough to endure (Mark 19:29; 10:30)." T. G. Soars, *The Social Institutions and Ideals of the Bible*, p. 317.

[7] Matt. 24:35.

In the Beatitudes Jesus sets forth the moral qualities that belong to the Kingdom. The virtues—humility, righteousness, patience, and the rest—which he there describes are the sound and steady qualities which were best in everyday living. It is just those qualities which make an individual a good man that fit him to be a member of the Kingdom. Humility is one of its chief traits. To enter the Kingdom one must become as a little child. Individual virtues and social virtues belong together. Jesus gives no ground for the pernicious notion that individual self-development and the development of society are mutually exclusive aims. To him the Kingdom is a kingdom of good men, a "realm of ends." Without such men there can never be industrial, economic or social redemption. And, on the other hand, as industrial and social conditions are bettered they will help men to be better.

Is this Kingdom a democracy? Yes, if democracy means a social order in which every individual has the opportunity to realize his best self in service. Why, then, call it a Kingdom? Because in it the will of God is supreme, although it is the will of a Father rather than a King. The "Kingdom of God," as used by Jesus, means the Divine rule; yet not of a Sovereign-God but of the Father-God.

(3) In Jesus' conception of the Kingdom the dividing line between those on this side of death and those on the other side loses definiteness and significance. The time element seems not to count for much in his mind. All

kinds of temporal paradoxes attach to his words concerning the Kingdom. It is *at hand* (Mark 1:15; Luke 10:9); it is *here,* among you (Luke 11:20); it is *coming* (Matt. 24:1-44; Mark 14:3-37). "The noble living and the noble dead" are sharers in its joys. Jesus is to drink wine with his disciples new in the Kingdom (Matt. 26: 29). This is to be after his death, but whether or not it is to be after their death does not appear. Nor is this joyous fellowship to be limited. On the contrary, not only will Abraham and Isaac and Jacob share in it, but "they shall come from the east and west and north and south and sit down together" in (Luke 13:28, 29) this redeemed society.

VI

Confusing and paradoxical as these descriptions appear, they are essentially germane to a Kingdom which is primarily a realm of personal relationships. In this realm life in time finds its meaning and value in affording scope and content to the eternal life of the spirit— which is both *in* time and *above* and *beyond* it. Such a Kingdom by its very nature is both present and future, imminent and delayed. It comes, as it were, both by growth and by the flash of revelation. It is as the seed and as lightning. It is both personal and social and draws within its compass all true souls in all ages. Place is no more part of its nature than time. It is "not here, nor there," but "within" (Luke 17:21). It is foolish to try to

locate it in Jerusalem, or anywhere else; for it is a state
of mind and heart incarnated in personal conduct and
relationships. It exists whenever and wherever the spirit
of Christ controls.

The temporal-eternal, social-spiritual nature of the
Kingdom might seem, at first thought, to make the obligation less urgent to go about establishing it here and
now. On the contrary, it serves as an incentive. As men
come to realize that the laws of a realm governed by a
righteous Father demand that social injustice and wrong
be rectified everywhere and at once, "and man to man
as brothers be and a' that and a' that," no advantages of
temporary enrichment will be sufficient to dazzle them
into disobedience to obligations which are so imperative
and so sacred.

Human brotherhood in the light of Divine Fatherhood,
on the one hand, reveals consequences certain and terrible, when violated, and, on the other, opens up a realm
of fellowship and coöperation which promises un-
dreamed-of good for coming generations issuing in a life
beyond time—and a' that and a' that.

CHAPTER XVI

The Fulfillment of the Faiths

The Fatherhood of God widely though dimly recognized among the Religions, yet clear and controlling only in Christianity—The Obligation to Sympathy and Service toward other Faiths which rests upon Christianity—Questions which the Orient is putting to Occidental Christianity; Counter-Questions and the Need of Discrimination—Obstacles to the Mission of Christianity decreasing; leaving the Way open for Christ to fulfill the religious Aspirations of Mankind.

I

THE dawn of belief in a Divine Father was world-wide before Christianity. His face appears in crude, anthropomorphic lineaments among the myths of savage races, and shines dimly, but with increasing clearness, through the loftier teachings of the greater religious faiths.[1] It could hardly be otherwise if religion is contact with a spiritual Reality which is personal. If we failed to find the conception of a Divine Father, however

[1] "It would not be untrue to say that every sincere and profound religion has found its highest point in a perception of the Divine-human relationship, or at least in a perception of those qualities in God which are now associated with the Christian term 'Father.'" Fred W. Morrow.

indistinct, appearing and reappearing throughout the religious experience of the race, we should be led to question its legitimacy in Christianity.

And yet, the fact remains that the Fatherhood of God is the *distinctive* teaching of but one religion. Nowhere, save in Christianity, does it stand out with clear, calm, unfaltering assurance. While it appears in other religions, occasionally, intermittently, as the sun breaks through intervening clouds, in Christianity alone it shines regnant and full-orbed. It has been greatly obscured, it is true, by internal discords and incongruous theological systems; but these, while they are a part of Christian history, have misrepresented true Christianity.

In spite of all the lapses from it, frequent and disheartening, the principle of the Fatherhood of God, as it is revealed in Christ, has always been the major and determining doctrine of the Christian faith. Inwrought into the life and teaching of Jesus, prominent in the faith of the apostles and in that of the fathers of the Church, avowed in the early creeds and confessions, the source of confidence even during the long periods of its partial eclipse, reappearing in fresh radiance in modern theology, Divine Fatherhood revealed in Christ has proven itself the life-giving and regulative principle of the Christian cults.

In so far as the doctrine of the Trinity has obscured it, that doctrine is being either repudiated or reinterpreted so as again to further the faith out of which it originally sprang. In so far as the doctrine of Divine Sovereignty

contradicts and belies it, the supremacy of the Sovereignty theology is losing its hold even upon those Christian bodies who still cling to the creeds in which it is
dominant. It is no mere sounding of brass or clanging of
cymbals to affirm that no other religion has within itself,
or has the power to convey, the conception of God as
Father in all the scope of its meaning and application
with anything like the convinced and convincing confidence of Christianity.[2]

The main reason for this is not far to seek. It is found
in Jesus Christ—not merely in his life and teaching but
in his *personality*. Explain it as one may, the incom-
parably transforming effect of this dynamic personality
upon human life and thought is demonstrated historic
fact. Where Christ gains a hold upon human thought
and life, there the Fatherhood of God becomes a vital,
puissant, working belief. It enters into all the avenues
of thought and conduct; it transforms nature and human
nature; it begets the exultant conviction: "Now are we
sons of God and it is not yet made manifest what we
shall be."

This power to make the Fatherhood of God a living
reality lays a strong, persistent, inescapable obligation
upon the Christian Church. It makes Christianity, by
the very compulsion of its nature, a missionary religion,

---

[2] There is a suggestive saying attributed to Thomas Arnold, which has
in it a large measure of truth, to the effect that while other religions
reveal men seeking God, only Christianity reveals God seeking men.
Of course, all religions reveal God seeking men, but the consciousness of
it becomes vivid only in Christianity.

feeling still the urge of Paul's cry, "Woe is me if I preach not the Gospel." The Gospel of the Fatherhood of God is proclaimed not so much by word of mouth as by communication of spirit. It may be denied utterance in speech and yet, when placed under the ban of silence, it can convey its message, as is now being done in Turkey, by daily deeds and the irresistible impress of Christlike love and goodwill. Denied one channel of expression, it will find another, and will not brook defeat.

II

What relationship does this peculiar endowment and message of Christianity create toward other faiths?

It gives birth, in the first place, to a consciousness of deep, spiritual kinship on the part of Christianity with other religions. To deny this kinship is to impugn the spirit of Christianity. "Though light has no fellowship with darkness, light does have fellowship with twilight," said John Henry Barrows, in Carnegie Hall, New York, in 1893, pleading in behalf of the Parliament of Religions.[3] For the truth of God as Father originates, as we have seen, not from a special revelation but from the common racial religious experience out of which all religions spring. This original revelation of the Spirit, this sense of "the Numinous," is primary, fundamental, universal; special revelation ensues upon it. Jesus Christ could never have persuaded men that God is their Father had

[3] Biography by his Daughter, p. 262.

the capacity for this truth not been already planted deep in the human soul. To hold to Universal Divine Fatherhood should involve, therefore, the readiness to recognize the kinship of all religions in which even its rudiments or its remnants appear.[4] In view of this fundamental relationship, *tolerance* is quite too negative and unfraternal an attitude toward other faiths. That which is common and consonant with Christianity in them constitutes a blood brotherhood which may not be dishonored. More than that. Whatever traits of true religion may be found in other faiths and not in Christianity, and whatever virtues and insights may be more fully developed in them than in Christianity, as it is practised in the West, call for incorporation into a larger Christianity. Christianity was born in the East. Who can doubt that hidden within it lie qualities and meanings which only the Eastern mind can understand and bring to full expression and fruition?

Nor can we stop here. Its peculiar realization of God as Father and its possession of Christ put upon Christianity the *obligation of supreme service*. The badge of that supremacy is not a miter, but a towel. There are two alternatives in the future adjustment of religions to one another: either a religious syncretism, made by blending many faiths into one, and hence a conglomerate and more or less nondescript product; or the *universalizing of Christianity*, in which the best in all faiths is taken up

[4] Probably there never has been so warm and inspiring an expression of the fellowship of religions as that of the Chicago Parliament of Religions already alluded to. See the two volumes of reports of the Parliament, edited by John Henry Barrows.

and fused in Christ. The latter is the only ideal which Christianity can further and be true to itself; for it is her conviction that Christ alone is able to harmonize, evaluate, unify, the faiths of mankind. If not he, what other? Confucius, Laotze, Mohammed, Gautama? The question answers itself. These are great names, but at no name will every creature bow save One, and to him only because he reveals, as no other does, the Universal Father.

Jesus Christ, as the supreme disclosure of Universal Fatherhood,—such is the faith of the Christian Church— is alone qualified and commissioned, by virtue of his moral and spiritual supremacy, to stand central and supreme among the religious prophets and leaders of the race. That, at least, is the major Christian conviction. To the Christian consciousness he is the consummate Flower of human faith, the Prophet of prophets, the perfect Avatar, the final Buddha, the Open Secret of creation, the purest Revelation of

"the God who framed
Mankind to be one mighty family,
Himself our Father, and the World our Home."
(S. T. Coleridge.)

This is not a dogma but an attitude of spirit. One may venture to believe that all the greatest spiritual leaders of the ages—could they be called upon for their attitude toward Christ—would freely and gladly confess him Lord and Master, even as those within Christendom itself have done. In such a fellowship of faith, one may

dare to think, would stand Abraham, father of the faith-
ful; Moses, lawgiver of Israel; Confucius, teacher of an
ethic that finds its culmination in the relation of father
and son; Laotze, expounder of the Way (Tao) which
leads to him who said, "I am the Way"; Socrates, critic
of the careless life and thirsting for righteousness; Plato,
exponent of the Word that in Christ became flesh; Zarathustra, battler for a righteousness which the Lord of
Lords wins for those who believe in Him; and, greatest of
all, Gautama, the Buddha, always turning the worship of
his followers away from himself, concerned only that men
should find enlightenment and the true way of salvation.
These all died in faith not having received the promise,
God having provided a better way that they without
Christ should not be made perfect.

III

The message of Universal Fatherhood through Christ,
welcome as it is bound to be, when purely presented, has
long been seriously impeded by the fact that Christian
nations in their dealing with non-Christian peoples have
so often belied the very principles which constitute the
foundation of their civilization. This has now become a
world scandal. There is no denying the indictment. It
is the shame and sorrow of true Christians. It is impossible to question the validity of the principle laid down by
our Lord: "By their fruits ye shall know them." Are
these, then, the fruits of Christian civilization: race dis-

crimination, commercial greed, secret diplomacy, armaments, patronage, hypocrisies? If so, the case is indeed
a forlorn one. But these are not the products of Christianity but of unsubdued human nature betraying Christianity. The sacrificial ministries of Christian teachers
and pastors and physicians—schools and hospitals and
services to the destitute and suffering—these are the true
and conclusive witness that Christians have had something at least of the spirit of Christ in their relations with
other peoples. If the peoples of the Orient could trace
the gifts for missions to the homes from which they come
and could know something of the sacrifice and prayer and
goodwill which prompt them, they would see something
of the true soul of Christianity. If governments and
armies and business monopolies misrepresent Christian
nations, must Christianity itself be implicated? It is
easy to understand, to sympathize with—and in a degree
to accept—the sharp distinction which the Orient is
making between Christianity and Christ; and yet there is
a true Christian civilization which, in spite of the para-
sites that cling to it, is entitled to its own germane and
worthy features.

Dean W. R. Matthews of London University in his
Boyle Lectures, *Studies in Christian Philosophy*, has presented a careful statement concerning the reality of a
Christian civilization and a striking analysis of its essence. "At least it may be said," he states, "that a genuine
Christian type of civilization exists in the same sense and
to the same degree as the true self of the individual. . . .

It exists as an ideal tendency, as a character emerging from confusion, struggling to be born. . . . These, then, seem to me to be the characteristic marks of the higher mind of Christian civilization. It is progressive and 'activist': it possesses a living unity: it has developed the ideal of freedom: it has invented the principle of universalistic humanism. And these are differentiating characteristics. In no other cultural mass are they so persistent. And, further, they are not independent of one another, but are interrelated so closely that we cannot help regarding them as aspects of a common spirit." [6]

May not we of the Occident ask our brothers of the Orient to discriminate between what Christianity really is and what those who live under its ægis, but have not its spirit, have made it appear to be? It would seem fair to expect them to make this discrimination. "But are you not, then,"—they rejoin,—"Christian nations? Is not America a Christian nation?" Yes and No. America is Christian in the purposes and spirit of its founders, Christian in its greatest leaders, men like Lincoln and John Hay and Roosevelt and Woodrow Wilson, but not Christian in many of its commercial dealings with other nations, not Christian in its diplomacy, its armaments, its gestures of hostility and aggrandizement.

"Why, then,"—the disconcerting question follows,— "has not Christianity made you Christian?" May we not answer with a counter-question: Why did not Buddhism make India Buddhist? Why did not Socrates make

[6] p. 63.

Greece Socratic, or Plato make it Platonist? Why has not Confucius made China Confucianist? Not because the teachings of these great leaders were at fault, but because the people as a whole did not respond to and realize the ideals presented to them. Nor will they respond to those of Christ to-day.

Yet the Orient has a further question to ask and one that stings: "You say that there is a vitality, a redemptive power in Christianity that the other faiths do not possess. *Why, then, has it not done for your people what our faiths have failed to do for us?*" What can we say to this? Nothing, but to admit: "The fault is ours, and it is humiliating, but do not lay it to our Faith, which but shines with the more rebuking light in contrast to our failure to be true to it."

Human nature is torpid, apathetic, reluctant to follow the best light that is given to it, slow to fulfill the ideals which it has accepted. That is why Europe and America are not more Christian. The fault, dear Orient, is not in our religion, but in ourselves, that we are still but selfish, half-Christian underlings.

IV

There is another serious inconsistency in Western Christianity, and one that stands out with peculiar flagrance in contact with other faiths, which, indeed, practically contradicts faith in "One God and Father"—*i.e.*, a divided Church. Disunion is becoming more shameful and full of reproach every day, as we face the task of world reconstruction. It cannot continue. The urge toward a United Church is felt to-day the world over. Stockholm, Lausanne, the United Church of Canada, the movements toward church union in India and China, mark the beginning of the end of the long era of alienation and division.

It is coming to be realized as never before that Christian unity is not a matter of creed or form of worship. Those who imagine that there can be no United Church until all think alike and worship alike are making a fatuous mistake. Christianity has proved in the past, more than once, the power of conscience to break away from organized corruption. The time has come for it to show the power of a great spiritual passion to weld divergent factions into one.

There is but one thing that the Church can do and be true to herself, and that is—not to call all other religions to her banner, but—to do her utmost to give to them Christ, confident that if he be lifted up he will draw all men unto himself. This is not a relationship of lordship but of service, not a claim of superiority but a fulfillment of duty, not a summons to the adherents of other faiths to give up anything that is really true and good, but a challenge to find it, in fuller meaning and worth, in Him in whom are hid all the treasures of wisdom and knowledge. Is Buddha dear to any? He will be dearer when seen through Christ. Is veneration for ancestors a part of any people's religion? It will become tenderer and truer, while less rigorous and perfunctory, in the Great Lover. Does any man believe that Allah is one Allah? He will believe it in a far larger way after seeing Him through Christ.

That religion which has the largest, most compelling, most redemptive conception of God and man, revealed through humanity's most spiritually vitalizing personality, must be, cannot but be, the interpreter, unifier, and fulfiller of the religions.

CHAPTER XVII

Conclusion

Our Discussion leaves many Difficulties unsolved; Nature remains an Enigma, yet no better Solution than Theism can be found; Humanity continues a Problem, yet not without Indications of Divine Descent—Personality, emerging from the Deeps of Nature and Spirit, and trained by taking Part in building the Moral Order, the Key of an Evolving Universe—The growing Recognition of Faith as a legitimate Means of reaching Truth; William James' Faith Ladder—Faith based on Experimental, as contrasted with Circumstantial, Evidence—An "on the whole" Judgment, gained by Intuition, supported by Faith, ratified by Reason and realized in Jesus Christ, a sufficient Ground for Confidence in the Fatherhood of God.

WE HAVE looked into—we can hardly say more—the belief in the Fatherhood of God, in search of its meaning and significance, as it has won the confidence of men through the life and teaching of Jesus. We have considered its power to convey the essence and values of Perfect Personality, its consonance with the principles of Theology, Philosophy, and Natural Science, and its harmony with mystical experience. We have faced, if not felled, some of the chief objections to it, arising through the problems of Natural and Moral Evil, of History and Providence. We have taken note of its effect in transforming life, in promoting human brotherhood and in relating Christianity to other faiths. It is to be hoped that as a result this yet unexhausted conception of God appears in somewhat more of its true clarity, reasonableness, and reality. And yet—how great the difficulties that remain.

I

It would be folly to presume that such a belief, even as a working hypothesis, could be easy for the modern mind. The universe, as it has unfolded itself to scientific investigation and philosophic reflection, is not susceptible to easy solution. The perplexing sum of experience has never readily lent itself to an inclusive interpretation— theistic, atheistic, pantheistic, agnostic, pluralistic, monistic, realistic, idealistic, naturalistic, or any other. And yet the mind calls for a solution. We submit that none better than Personal Theism can be found.

If Nature is an enigma, humanity is not less so. Is it good or bad? Does it give indication of being spiritual and heaven-born or only gross and earth-born? To survey humanity as a whole in order to determine whether it is such as to point toward God as its Father is manifestly absurd. The limited part of its vast totality, present and past, which can be observed presents such confusions and contradictions as leave one perplexed and baffled. Can God be the Father of a race whose history has been so blackened by savagery, slavery, cannibalism, war, polygamy, crime, ignorance, which, even in its "civilized" estate, has witnessed the Dark Ages, the Inquisition, the Thirty Years' War, industrial slavery, commercialized vice, the drink evil, the Great War? Yet, on the other hand, can a race that has emerged from savagery, that has cast off slavery, rejected polygamy, attained to some degree of religious toleration, been inspired to write a Bible, a *Bhagavad Gita,* a *Divina Commedia,* that has created art and science, built cathedrals, established tribunals of justice, that is warring against vice and crime and drink, and is now struggling toward industrial freedom and the abolition of war—can such a race be understood apart from a Purposeful, Guiding Spirit above and within it? There is much to make one regard humanity with distress if not with disgust.

> "[But] wiser he, whose sympathetic mind
> Exults in all the good of all mankind."

If the misanthrope asks: Why so many men who live as if there were no Divine Father? it is pertinent to ask the counter-question: *Why so many who live as if there were?* Who does not know virtuous and resplendent characters no more to be accounted for without Divine origin and sustenance than the flowers on the hillside without the sun? One meets them everywhere—on city streets and country roads and forest trails, in shops and factories and offices, in academic, business, and church circles, filling large places and humble—and knows them at once as children of God, wearing the nimbus of spiritual radiance that attests their birth and fealty. To encounter such is to gain fresh faith in a Fatherly God. Granted that they are in the minority—perhaps only a remnant—how account for this "saving remnant"?

II

We are accustomed to the injunction to "look at both sides" of a question. But having seen them, as far as may be, the question ensues: *Are both sides equally meaningful? If not, which side is the significant side, the positive side, in whose light we may look at the whole understandingly? On which side is the lock?*

There is one signal outcome and issue of this "thick-crowded, inextricably intertwined hieroglyphic writing" —to use Carlylean language—in which we find ourselves, to which attention should once more be called, which promises to explain, in part at least, its mysteries and justify its striving and suffering, perhaps to require them, and thus to prove the key to the whole, and that is *the emergence and development of personality.* With all its apparent aimlessness and imperfection, this is a *personality-producing,* or rather, a *personality-training,* universe.

> "Out of the deep
> Where all that was to be, in all that was,
> Whirl'd for a million æons thro' the vast
> Waste dawn of multitudinous-eddying light—"

has emerged this Wondrous Worth—the *person*, conscious, intelligent, free, self-directive,

"Breaking with laughter from the dark."
"For in the world, which is not ours, They said
'Let us make man' and that which should be man,
From that one light no man can look upon,
Drew to this shore lit by the suns and moons
And all the shadows. O dear Spirit half-lost
In thine own shadow and this fleshly sign
That thou art thou—who wailest being born
And banish'd into mystery, and the pain
Of this divisible-indivisible world
Among the numerable-innumerable
Sun, sun, and sun, thro' finite-infinite space
In finite-infinite Time—our mortal veil
And shatter'd phantom of that infinite One,
Who made thee unconceivably Thyself
Out of His whole World-self and all in all—
Live thou! and of the grain and husk, the grape
And ivyberry, choose; and still depart
From death to death thro' life and life, and find
Nearer and ever nearer Him, who wrought
Not Matter, not the finite-infinite,
But this main-miracle, that thou art thou,
With power on thine own act and on the world." [1]

Spirit, selfhood, freedom, development—a Moral Order: Is the poet right in discerning these? If so, why is the Moral Order so indecisive and incomplete? The answer—one answer at least—is that *we are here to take part in completing it.* "The best world for a moral

[1] Tennyson, *De Profundis*.

agent," as Professor Royce has said, "is one that needs him to make it better." [2]   Whether it *can* be made better or not, *the person who tries to make it so is made better.* In other words, the person is self-made—at least in part. But only in part; that he himself knows. For if there is anything of which one who thinks at all is sure it is that Something besides himself has brought him, as well as the world about him, into being. What is It? Who is It? Is this "main-miracle" of the person "with power on his own act and on the world" a "shattered phantom of the infinite One," or is he a mere sport, an *epiphenomenon,* breaking with curious inconsequence from an unconscious Nature? Thus we are thrust back once more, at the very end of our discussion, to face the initial problem: *Is there a Fatherly God?*

III

It is impossible to prove conclusively the existence of God, much more His Fatherhood. That was conceded at the outset of our discussion and is reaffirmed at the close. Yet that does not invalidate the conviction itself. Proof is not the kind of certification that is germane in the realm of moral and spiritual experience. The mystery and complexity of human life and of the cosmos are too great for complete intellectual solution. Every new "discovery" of science, every fresh conjecture of philosophy, adds to the difficulty of the problem of Ultimate

[2] *The World and the Individual,* II, p. 341.

Reality and to the deepening conviction that there is no solution except that reached through *intuitive adventure,* or what Professor D. C. McIntosh has called "moral optimism," [3] *i.e.,* faith.

"Every thinker takes his life in his hand, the denier no less than the affirmer," writes George A. Gordon. The truth of this statement becomes more evident the more the horizon widens. It would seem better worth while, other things being equal, to take one's life in his hand for an affirmation than for a negation. "But that is trusting one's desire," some one will say. Perhaps; but it is more reasonable to trust one's normal desires than to distrust them. One trusts his desire for food and drink, for fellowship and beauty, and is not cheated—why not his desire for God? "The idea of the Fatherhood of God is rooted in religious experience. Those who have had that experience know that the conception is true, truer than any other. Those who have not had the experience will disbelieve it." [4]

Philosophy never gave just consideration, until William James' *The Will to Believe,* to what religion calls *faith,* either as a method of realizing truth or as a way of meeting life. Since that time the part which the outreach of the mind plays in making truth real has received increasing recognition. A recent volume, *Problems of Belief,* by F. C. S. Schiller, closes thus: "At the core of being there is always found a *value-judgment* which ap-

[3] Cf. *The Reasonableness of Christianity.*
[4] Mrs. Martha Usteri Appia.

proves the reality it acknowledges. It is never a mere acceptance of a 'given,' but always an interpretation which selects, and rejects, 'appearances.' And its intention is prophetic. It is justified, or falsified, by the consequences it entails. Thus the all-pervasive presence of a final act of Faith may never be omitted from a survey of beliefs." Sir Henry Jones' *A Faith that Enquires* and L. P. Jacks' *The Faith of a Worker* emphasize faith.[5]

In the appendix of William James' posthumous *Some Problems of Philosophy* will be found a very significant *addendum* to his essay on *The Will to Believe,* entitled *Faith and the Right to Believe.* An extract from it follows:

. . . Philosophy and Religion have to interpret the total character of the world, and it is by no means clear that here the intellectualist postulates obtain. It may be true all the while (even though the evidence be still imperfect) that, as Paulsen says, 'the natural order is at bottom a moral order.' It may be true that work is still doing in the world-process, and that in that work we are called to bear our share. The character of the world's results may in part depend upon our acts. Our acts may depend on our religion,—on our not-resisting our faith-tendencies, or on our sustaining them in spite of 'evidence' being incomplete. These faith-tendencies in turn are but expressions of our good-will towards certain forms of result.

Such faith-tendencies are extremely active psychological

[5] So also Viscount Haldane: "It is only with what we sometimes call the eye of faith, the realization of things unseen, that we can behold God, but religion and art alike tell us that such a faith can sustain us." Quoted by M. C. Ott, *Journal of Philosophy,* xxiv, 3, p. 82.

forces, constantly outstripping evidence. The following steps
may be called the 'faith-ladder':

1. There is nothing absurd in a certain view of the world
being true, nothing self-contradictory;

2. It *might* have been true under certain conditions;

3. It *may* be true, even now;

4. It is *fit* to be true;

5. It *ought* to be true;

6. It *must* be true;

7. It *shall* be true, at any rate for *me*. . . .

Faith thus remains as one of the inalienable birthrights of
our mind. Of course it must remain a practical, and not a
dogmatic attitude. It must go with toleration of other faiths,
with the search for the most probable, and with the full consciousness of responsibility and risks.

It may be regarded as a formative factor in the universe, if
we be integral parts thereof, and co-determinants, by our behavior, of what its total character may be.

IV

It is by no means necessary to start with a *pluralistic
universe* in order to reach Theism by means of the "faith-
ladder." It is to be used, as James points out, not in
order to reach *any* desired conclusion, but only such as
are not absurd or contradictory and are *fit* and *ought* to
be true. In other words, one starts with a rational principle—such as the existence of a good God—and mounts
the faith-ladder not to find it or prove it, but to
realize it.

As a matter of fact, faith is in constant and reliable

use in all our personal relations, and the failure to exercise it means impotence and disaster. Perhaps no better illustration of the latter result could be instanced than that of Othello in his tragic distrust of Desdemona. Two kinds of evidence were before Othello—what is called "circumstantial evidence" and experiential evidence. Everything which goes to make up a common-sense judgment, or the decision of a case in court, was against Desdemona. Yet, on the other hand, there was a kind of evidence in her favor which should have outweighed for Othello the whole force and circumstance of damaging testimony—*i.e.*, the personal knowledge of her and of her loyalty, of which he had ample measure had he trusted it. This is the sort of knowledge that the author of Hebrews calls "the evidence of things not seen"; invisible, intangible, yet wholly sound and reliable. Because he refused to honor it Othello was guilty of the tragic, heinous blunder that Shakespeare has pictured with such vivid and heart-breaking realism.

This kind of knowledge, "evidence of things not seen," faith, is precisely that which generates and sustains all true and dependable relationships between persons, including ourselves and God. It is this alone which can stand against the tide of appearances which is always flooding in to destroy family ties, friendships, and all the fealties of the personal order. We either learn to cherish confidence in each other and live in love, or fall into mistrust and misery and die in isolation.

There is a deep-seated testimony to moral and spiritual

realities which witness to their integrity by "bearing it out even to the verge of doom" in support of them. No philosophy that belittles this kind of testimony to reality can be other than academic and *dilettante*. Reliance upon spiritual verities may appear to be mere idealism, Quixotism, sentimentalism, yet in the end prove to be the only road to Ultimate Reality. To believe in God as Father is to go with reason, as far as it goes and then beyond it, but not against it.

Christian Theism is as reasonable, defensible, and well tested an interpretation of Ultimate Reality as any other. Indeed, no other presents *on the whole* so intrepid, rational, and livable a solution of the problem of existence.

V

That judicious and comprehensive phrase "on the whole," which thoughtful minds so often use, is full of genuine wholesomeness. Of course, it does not mean that the whole can be surveyed; for that is just what cannot be done. To survey the whole of Nature and human life would require the all-comprehending time-span of which Professor Royce has written so illuminatingly in his *The World and the Individual*. The human mind is limited; yet it is significant that it can conceive of an all-inclusive, Eternal Mind, and then refer the limitations of the finite viewpoint to that Mind. This is at once an act of reason and an act of faith.

Although "on the whole" cannot mean a view of the

whole, it may mean a *whole view* as concerns that segment of human experience, vouchsafed to each of us, which in some degree reflects the whole. Such a segment, embosomed in the whole, may be viewed with a judgment and an insight into its meaning which enable one to reach an intelligent conclusion. In this way, "seeing life steadily and seeing it whole," as far as it is given us to do, I think we may say, reasonably, sanely, defensibly, daringly, that this is God's world and that the modern man's religious problems, difficult as they are, are by no means sufficient to obscure His Fatherhood.

If the intellectual difficulties in the way of Theism are great, they are no greater, let it be repeated, than are met with in any other life-philosophy. Let one adopt and undertake to defend any of the nontheistic philosophies —Atheism, Pantheism, Materialism, Agnosticism, Naturalism—and what problems roll in upon him, what experiences overflow the bounds of his theory, what questions he finds himself unable to answer, what objections arise that he cannot meet! It is so with every universal philosophy. The universe calls for an interpretive philosophy—and then tears it to shreds, as a flag is torn in the wind. One who would explore the orb of Truth finds himself obliged to sail past the Gates of Hercules, out upon an unknown sea. And yet it is a sea overshadowed by a Presence. For, as Pascal perceived, one could not seek God if he had not already found Him.

"This is the best of impossible worlds!" exclaims Chesterton, in one of his rollicking, rational-irrational hyperboles. Christianity with its faith in the Fatherhood of God is as impossible and as possible, as unreasonable and as reasonable, now as it has ever been. If it has to meet fresh obstacles it has fresh means with which to meet them. If many new facts elude the Christian faith, many sustain it. If it requires fresh courage, it gains thereby fresh strength. As James Ward—than whom no philosopher of our time has spoken with more maturity of judgment—wrote, just before his death:

> There is, then, as Kant has shewn, room for the faith in God, which is for religion a perennial source of confidence that the Supreme Good is assured, a confidence which for radical empiricism is avowedly lacking. But what is here meant by faith is not that our reflexions have brought us to entertain the existence of God as a more or less probable hypothesis, with which as Laplace maintained, science can dispense. This faith is not an opinion, which meanwhile may eke out a gap in our knowledge that is still awaiting unification. It is rather a certain trustfulness, (pistis) of a kind which is implicit throughout life and makes knowledge itself first of all possible.[6]

Something there is, or Some One, besetting man behind and before—that is too deep-rooted a conviction to be easily set aside—Something besides the external world— "Something More," as William James called it. Whatever or Whoever It is, It is the Great Reality, as inescapable as It is reassuring, producing at once the dim dread, the awe, and also the fascination and joy, of the Numinous. "The drift of pinions would we hearken beats

[6] J. H. Muirhead, *Contemporary British Philosophy*, Vol. II, p. 53.

at our clay-shuttered doors." To emergent man this Awesome Thing invested mountain, river, tree, totem. It stimulated the wild incoherence of the shaman and the ordered incantations of the priest. It impelled man to sacrifice everything—the fruits of his toil, the beasts of forest and field, even his own offspring—to It, at times stirring him to all kinds of frenzied excitement, yet in the end quieting, inspiring, reassuring him and yielding the peaceable "fruits of the spirit."

What is It? Who is He? Every possible answer has been offered, every conceivable concept, name, idea, symbol, for It has been seized. Yet none suffices. Is this Some One the creation of man's imagination? Say rather the creator of it. Is It Many—a throng of spirits, invisible, ubiquitous, fearsome, needing to be placated and appeased, or a family of gods, dwelling in the forest aisles or on Olympus, or at local shrines and temples, and appearing at rare moments to chosen individuals? This answer served long—yet did not suffice. Both spiritism and polytheism had their day and ceased to be. The spirits vanished before the wand of science. The scepters of the gods fell from lifeless hands. Olympus still rises into the clouds, but empty of its company of immortals; the thunder rolls about its heights, but it is no longer the voice of Zeus, father of gods and men. Advancing reflection sought a more rational explanation than polytheism could give.

Is the Invisible Reality, then, the *One*, the *All?* Speculation and contemplation seem to have reached their apotheosis in this conception. Yet it also fails to satisfy, for experience outruns it. Expansive and impressive as is the Whole, it is only—the Whole. The mind yearns for Some One above and beyond it. It does not answer to the sense of the Sacred. Quantity, the Whole has in superabundance, but the *quality* which religion requires It has not.[7] The Whole does not inspire or satisfy worship.

Is "the many-splendoured Thing" *Nature?*—the Bountiful, the Beautiful, the Absorbing—Nature which kindles the flame of desire and satisfies it, the Source of Life, the Joy of the poet, the artist, the lover, and the inexhaustible Resource of the scientist? Once more, experience answers, No. The Numinous pervades, hallows, glorifies Nature but is not itself Nature. Nature is *Nature,* inciting worship but not worshipful, pointing to the Ultimate but not itself the Ultimate.

Is the *About-to-be* the Numinous? Is Deity evolving? Is the "Something More" which awakens reverence and will not let us go, that which is just Beyond—coming into being as the Next, perhaps the Last, great Emergent in the creative, developmental process? [8] This latest and most daring interpretation of the Numinous too falls short of satisfying religious experience. For it is not Something yet to be that haunts the soul but *Something that has*

[7] For the distinction between quantity and quality, as related to religion, see H. B. Streeter, *Reality.*

[8] Cf. S. Alexander, *Space, Time and Deity.*

always been and is and is to be, manifold in manifestation but eternal in essence.

Can it be, then, *Humanity itself* that is really God, the quest ending where it begins—in Man? Is he himself, in his yet unrealized powers, the Sacred, the Numinous, the Worshipful?

That is the conclusion to which certain minds have come. But not many. For the goal is not here. Humanity is—*humanity,* great and noble in its virtues, its capacities, its aspirations and achievements, but finite in its powers, pitiful in its weakness, ever conscious of incompleteness—the son of God, but not God. It is significant that those who have attained the highest achievements in virtue and honor have been the foremost to cry: "Not unto us, not unto us ——" That is the voice of humanity as a whole.

Thus we return to the conception with which we started —simple to comprehend but boundless in scope, lowly in origin but rich in symbolic meaning and value—our Father. The Numinous is best conceived as like a Father—like as a Father pitying his children—like a Father, creative and life-giving, transcendent and immanent, of the "same nature" as his offspring, yet infinitely above them, the Perfect Person, the Great Companion.

This is the nearest men have been able to come to a satisfying concept of God—simple yet ever expanding, including and harmonizing the highest metaphysical and metaphorical conceptions of Deity, embracing the ninety-nine beautiful names in a single rosary, yet leading all the rest. Let one trust his intuition and climb William James' ladder of faith and he will find such a God; let him remain on the level of his lower nature, indifferent or self-sufficient, and no God of any kind is to be found.

If there were a human relationship transcending fatherhood in fitness, wealth, and warmth of meaning, to serve as a better symbol, there might be a better name for God than Father. Since there is not, progress in the conception of Him lies in broadening and deepening the meanings that lie yet unrealized within this truly beautiful and sufficient symbol (without excluding others), as its implications—experiential, cultural, and philosophical—are developed.

There is One who is unwilling, yet willing, to be called Father—implicit in religious experience, discerned by intuition, apprehended by faith, approved by reason, known by love, revealed in him who taught us to pray, saying: "Our Father who art in Heaven."

Index

Abraham, 225
 influence, 40
Absolutism, defects, 88
Addresses on Religion, Friedrich
 Schleiermacher, 76
Aeneid, Virgil, 173
Æschylus, Zeus called father, 43
Agassiz, Louis, religious spirit, 99
Agnosticism, 104
 defects, 109
Ahkenaton, influence, 40
Alexander, H. B., philosophy of
 personality, 94
Alexander, Samuel, agnostic real-
 ism, 106
 on the numinous, 245, *note*
Allen, Ethan, on rationalism, 77
Anabaptists, 211
Analects, Confucius, 173
Analogy, Joseph Butler, 77
Animals, friends of, 144 *et seq.*
 sacrifice justified, 145 *et seq.*
 suffering caused by humans, 144
 religions and, 144 *et seq.*
 societies to protect, 145
Animism, in religion, 34, *note*
Animism, George W. Gilmore, 35,
 note
Antiquary, The, Scott, 174
Apologia, Cardinal Newman, 174
Apology, Plato, 173
Appia, Mrs. Martha Usteri, on
 divine fatherhood, 237, *note*
Aquinas, St. Thomas, mysticism, 89
 on benevolence of God, 60

Aristotle, idea of God, 85
 on reproduction, 152
 philosophy of personality, 93
Arminianism, 75
Arnold, Thomas, on Christianity,
 221, *note*
Assyria, reason for decay, 161
Atlantic Monthly, notes on 31,
 112, 178, 189
Augustine, St., concepts of God,
 73 *et seq.*
 mysticism, 121
 on benevolence of God, 60
 on God's will, 183
 on the philosophy of history,
 167
 on the Trinity, 32
 theology, 73
 thought provoking writings, 115
Avatemasaka Sutra, 141, *note*

Babylon, reason for decay, 161
Bacon, Benjamin, on the historic
 Jesus, 80, *note*
Bacon, Francis, theism, 99
Bacon, Roger, correspondence with
 Pope Clement IX, 99
Barnes, Albert, on a theology of
 experience, 76
Barrows, John Henry, on the
 Parliament of Religions, 222
Beecher, Henry Ward, on a
 theology of experience, 76
Benedict, St., mysticism, 121
Benedictines, 211

Fabre, J. H., on animal instinct, 137

Faerie Queene, The, Spenser, 174

Fairbairn, Andrew M., on Christocentric theology, 81

Faith, a cherished heritage, 14
basis of moral order, 204
effects of, 195 *et seq.,* 200 *et seq.,* 209
fulfillment of, 219-230
views of, 237
what it is, 8

Faith of a Worker, The, L. P. Jacks, 238

Faith that Enquires, A, Sir Henry Jones, 88, *note;* 238

Family, based on divine, 205
danger to modern, 205

Faraday, Michael, religious spirit, 99

Father, as a term for God, 25, 42 *et seq.,* 118 *et seq.*
Biblical use of, 44
substitute terms, 95, 96, 113, 116, 118

Fatherhood of God, 13
a distinctive Christian teaching, 220
as fostered by philosophy, 83-96
as perfect personality, 55-65
a symbol, 27-41
belief difficult for modern mind, 14-26, 232
disclosed by Christ, 224
early conceptions, 85, 219
enlargement of idea necessary, 176
foreshadowings of idea, 43
Gospel teaching, 53
gratitude for, 201 *et seq.*
human brotherhood and, 207 *et seq.*
immanence of, 50, 79 *et seq.*
life and the, 195-206
mysticism of, 111-122

Fatherhood of God—(*Continued*)
natural science and, 97-110
philosophy and, 83-96
progress in conception of, 247
sonship revealed, 42-54
source of family, 205
supremacy of love, 49
taken seriously by Jesus, 44
the infinite personality, 94
theology and, 69-82

Fawcett, Douglass, on creation, 63

Feeling (*see* Emotion)

Ferishtah's Fancies, Robert Browning, 174

Fiske, John, on the struggle for existence, 143

Flewelling, R. T., philosophy of personality, 94

Fosdick, Harry Emerson, on Christian conscience and war, 14, *note*

Fox, John, mysticism, 122

Francis, St., friendliness to animals, 144
mysticism, 122
on God's will, 185

Franciscans, 211

Frank, on a theology of experience, 76

Franklin, Benjamin, on rationalism, 77

Friends, Society of, 5
term for God, 117

Froude, James A., on moral foundation of the world, 160

Galileo, reverence, 99

Galsworthy, John, on Joseph Conrad, 127

Gandhi, Mahatma, on the living Christ, 199

Garrison, William Lloyd, anti-slavery agitation, 212

Gilmore, George W., on animism, 35, *note*

INDEX

l 259

Paul, St.—(*Continued*)
on God's will, 185
on inner power of man, 139-140
on prayer, 205
on preaching the gospel, 222
on providence, 174
on spiritism, 34
philosophy of history, 167
philosophy of personality, 93
sovereignty theory, 75
teaching about Jesus, 52
terms for the divine, 117
Paine, Thomas, a social reformer, 210
on rationalism, 77
Palmer, George Herbert, xiv
on Shakespeare, 164
philosophy of personality, 93
Parables, Jesus' teaching in, 29
Paradise Lost, John Milton, 171
Parkman, Francis, on Indian religion, 40
Pascal, Blaise, on providence, 174
on seeking God, 242
on the perfections of nature, 136
Pater, Walter, on the divine presence, 197
Paterson, W. P., on the nature of religion, 138, *note*
Peake, A. S., on nature-worship, 38, *note*
on the historic Jesus, 80, *note*
Pearson, Karl, evidence of the senses, 107
Pelagianism, 75
Pensées, Joseph Joubert, 110, *note*
Pensées, Pascal, 174
Personalism, concept of God, 94
evolution, 93-94
Personalism, Bowne, 94
Personality, perfect, 55-65
as an abstraction, 56
creation inherent in, 60 *et seq.*
God as, 58 *et seq.*
philosophical concept of God, 64

Personality and Psychology, John Wright Buckham, 106, *note*
Personality and the Christian Ideal, John Wright Buckham, 94, *note*
Phaedrus, Plato, 115
Phillips, Wendell, anti-slavery agitation, 212
Philosophy, and the conception of God as Father, 83-96
common sense as, 84
contrasted with theology, 85
defects, 111
function as opposed to religion, 95
personality in modern, 93 *et seq.*
primary interest, 84
three great systems, 86
Philosophy of Personalism, The, A. C. Knudson, 94, *note*
Philosophy of Religion, Henry Calderwood, 91, *note*
Philosophy of Religion, Harald Höffding, *notes on* 29, 114, 208
Pietism, 77
Pilgrim's Progress, John Bunyan, 115
Place of Death in Evolution, The, Newman Smyth, 150
Plato, idea of God, 85
mysticism, 115
on mythology, 36
on providence, 173
on the Creator, 139
philosophy of personality, 93
Platonists, Cambridge, mysticism, 122
Plotinus, concept of God, 87
rationality, 115
Pope, Alexander, on coöperation in nature, 143
Positivism, 86
divine concept, 89
naturalism, 90